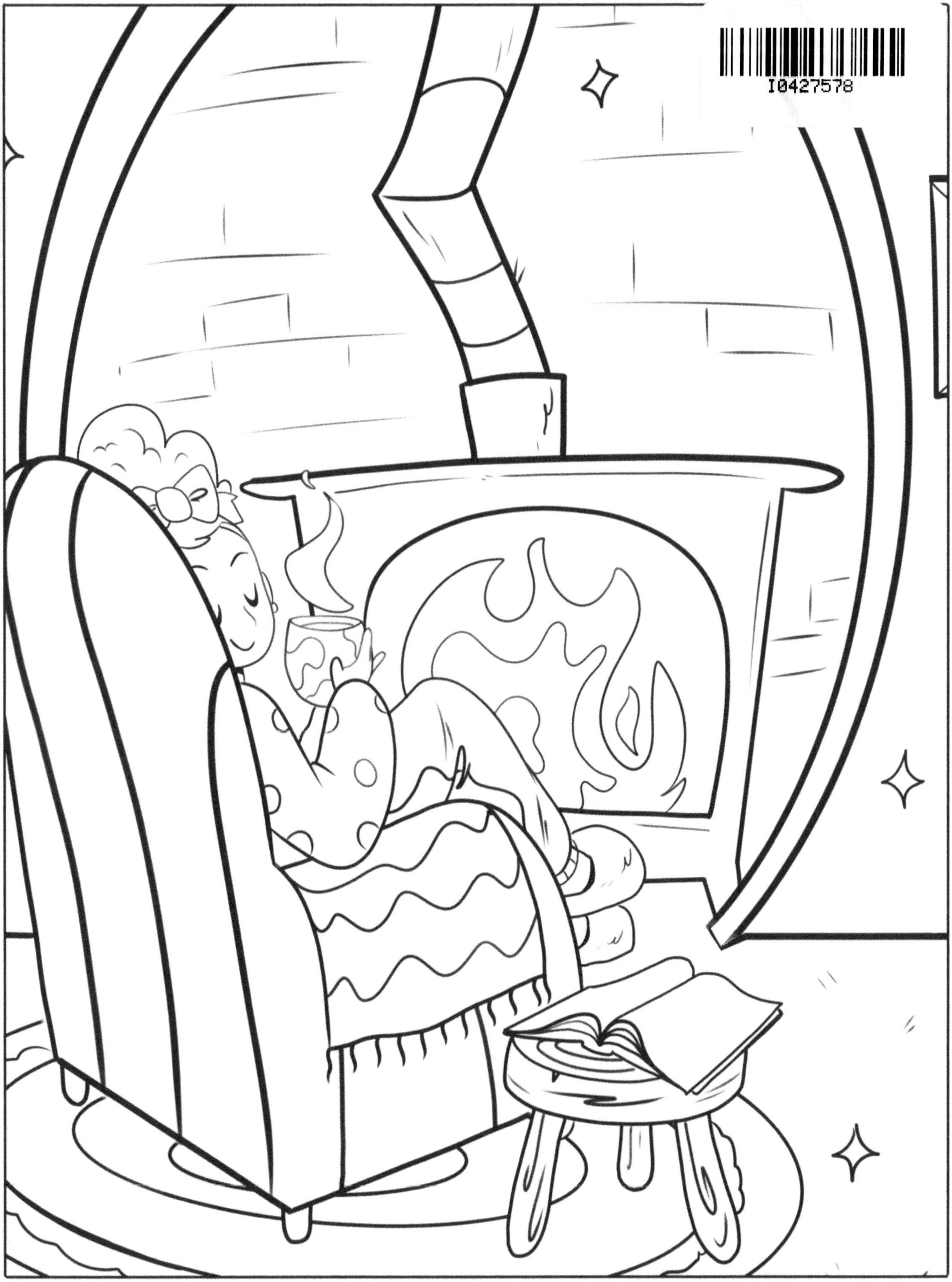

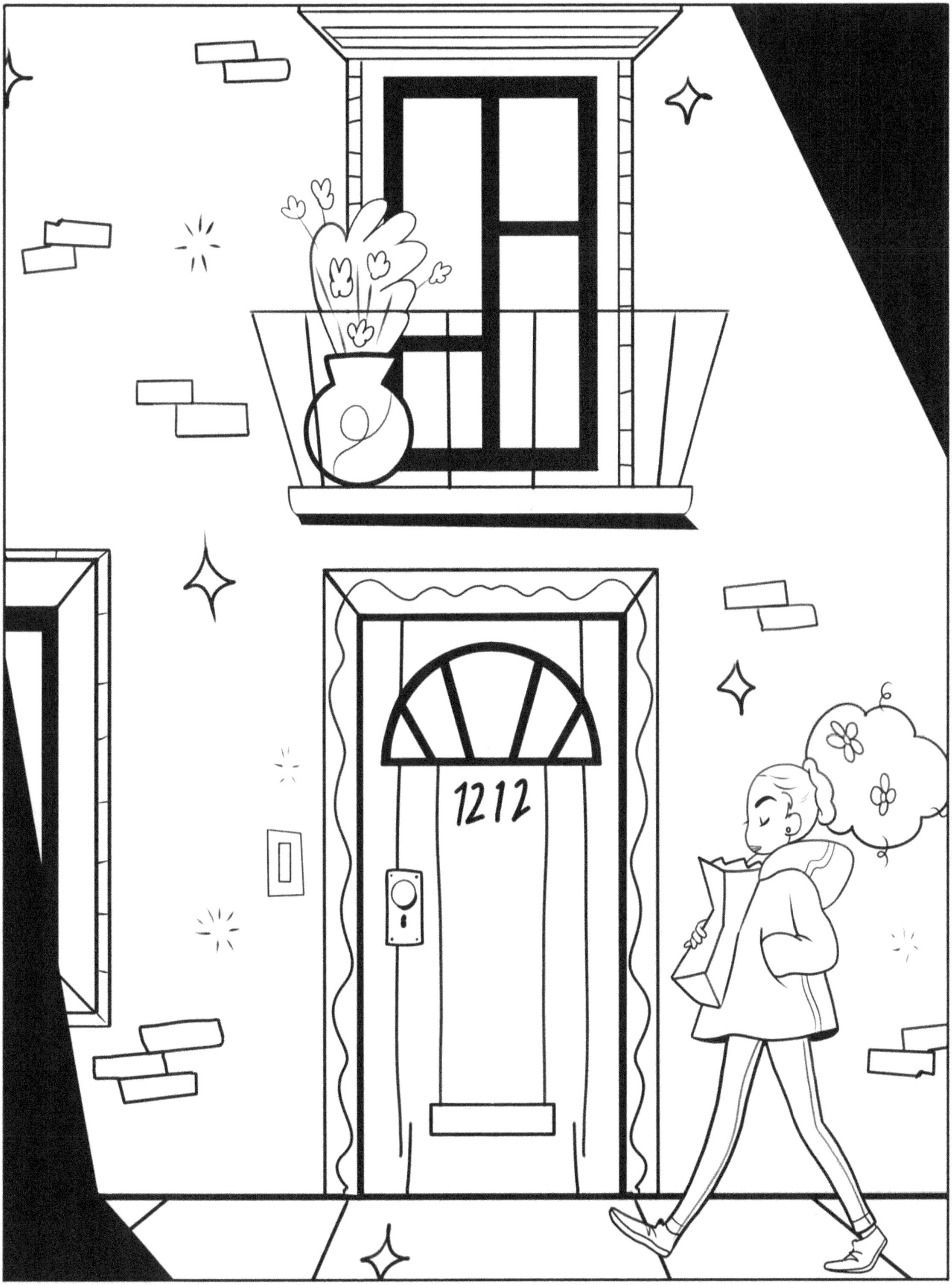
1212

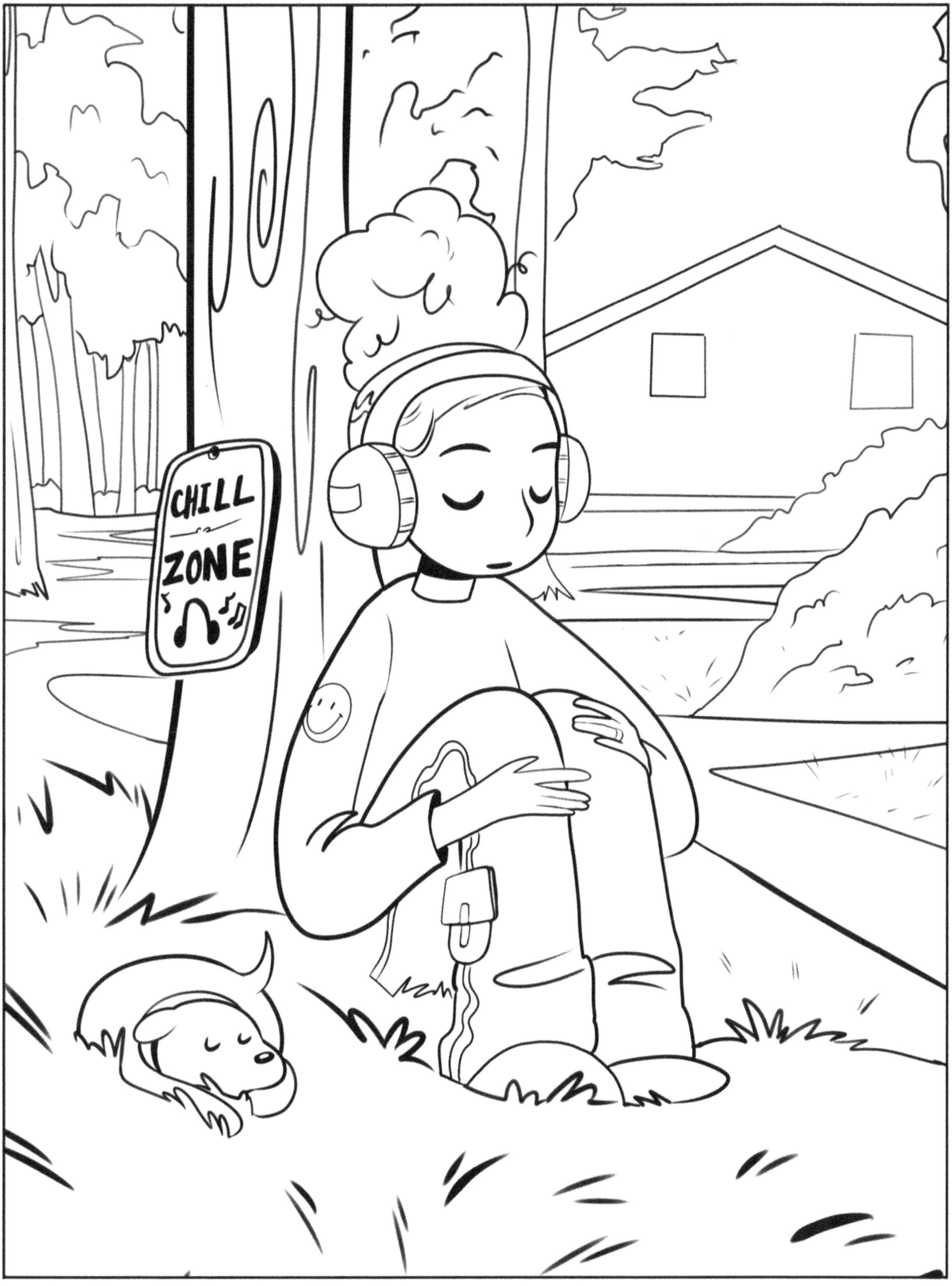
CHILL
ZONE

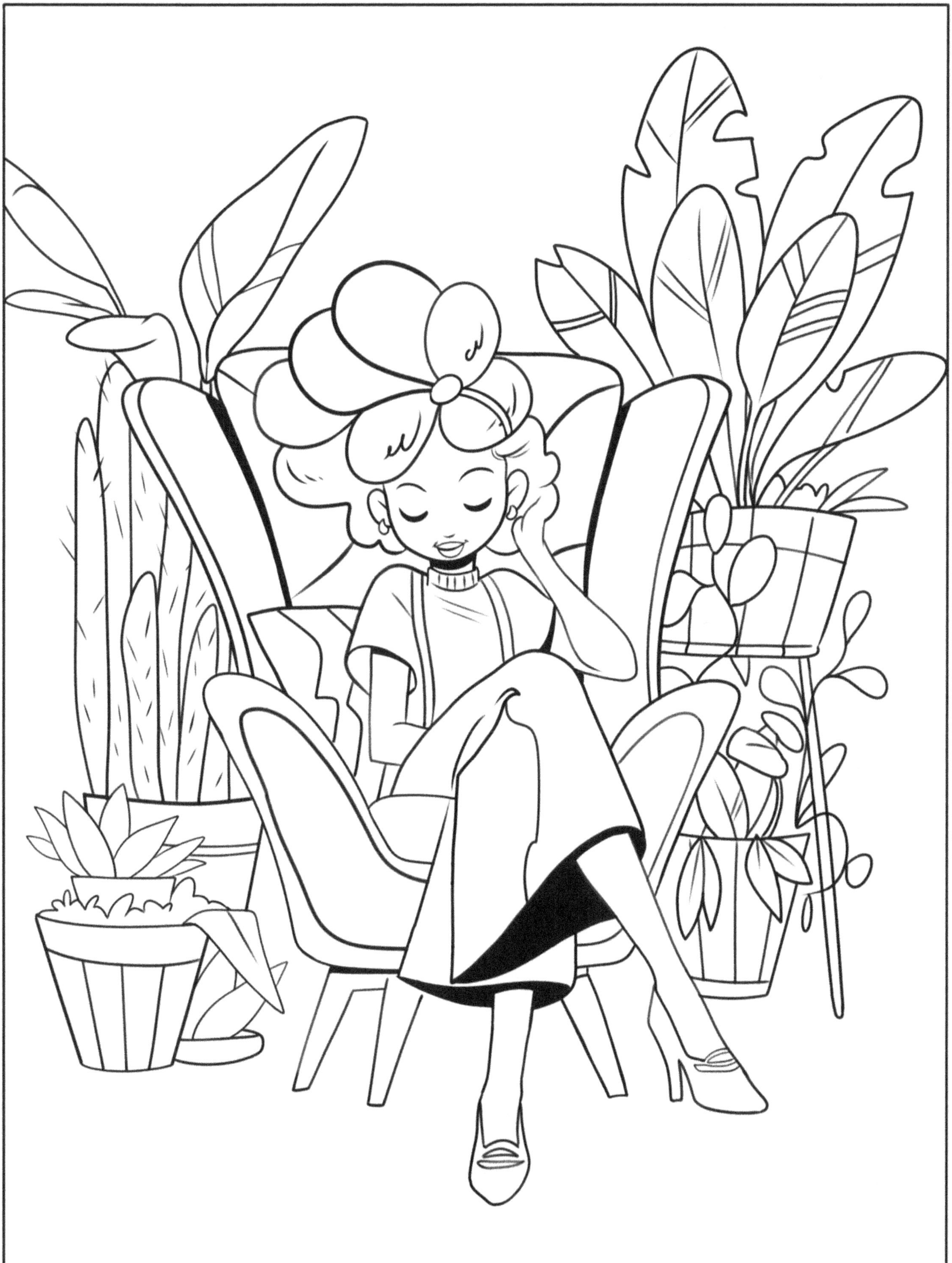

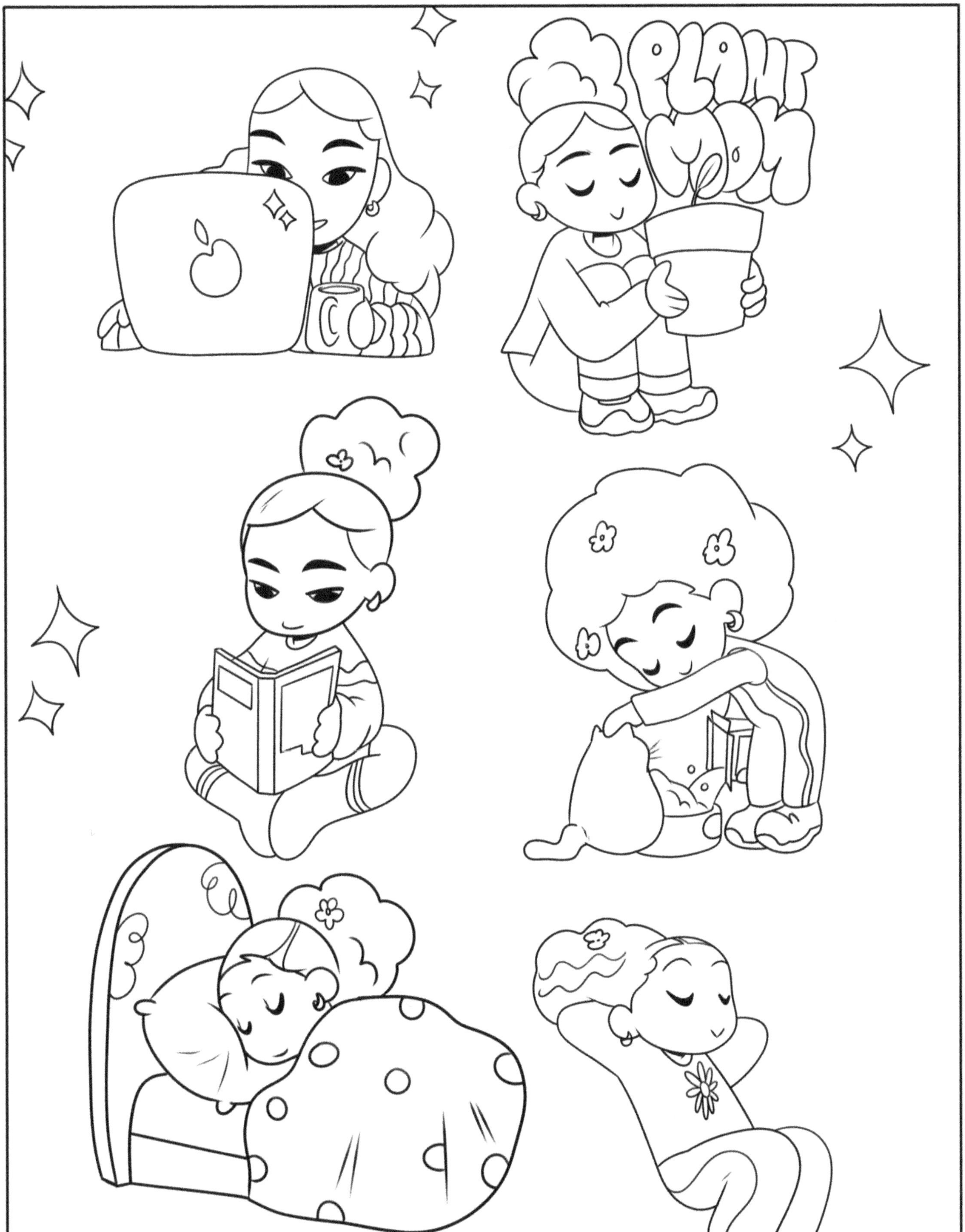
PLANT MOM

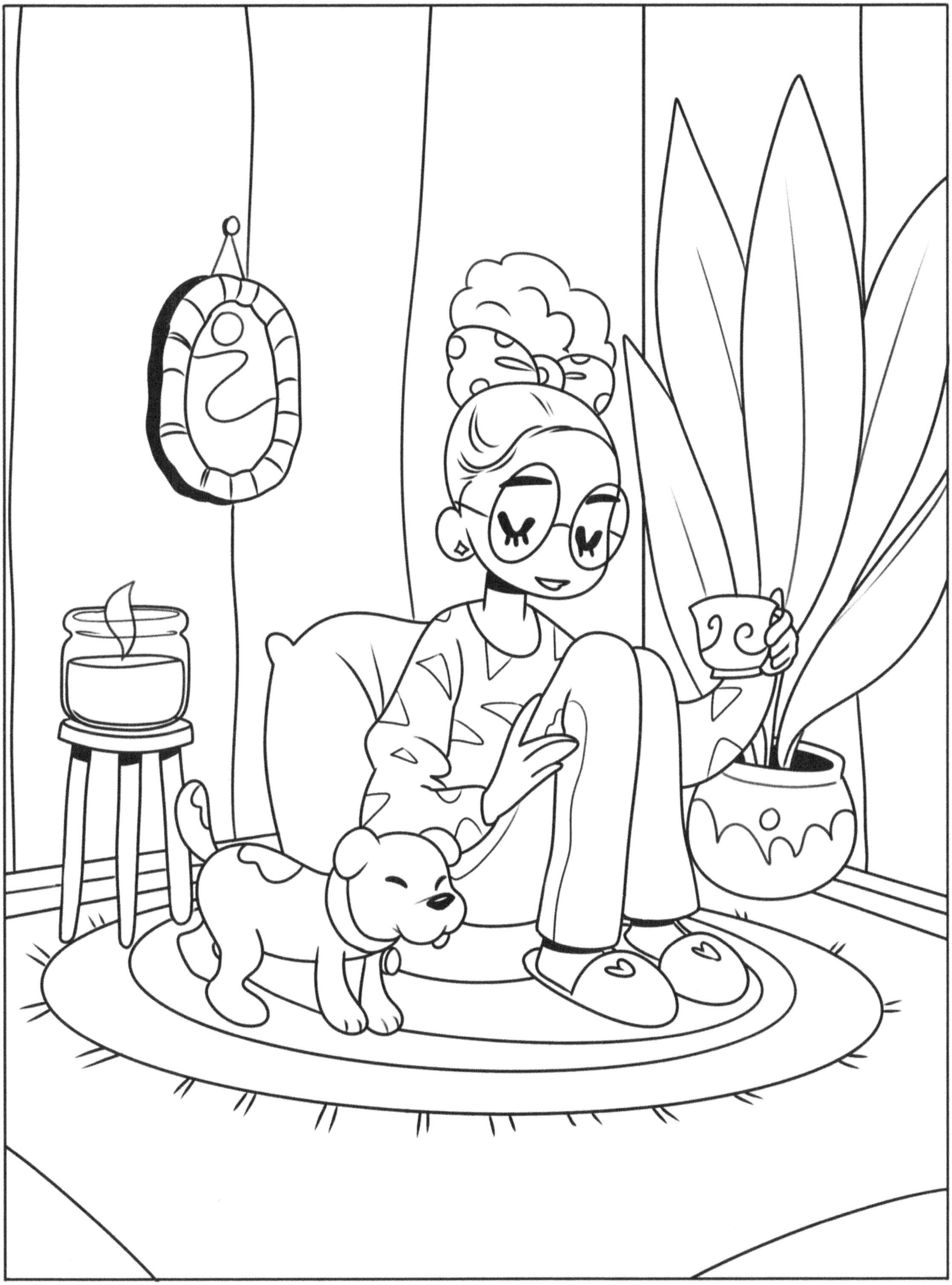

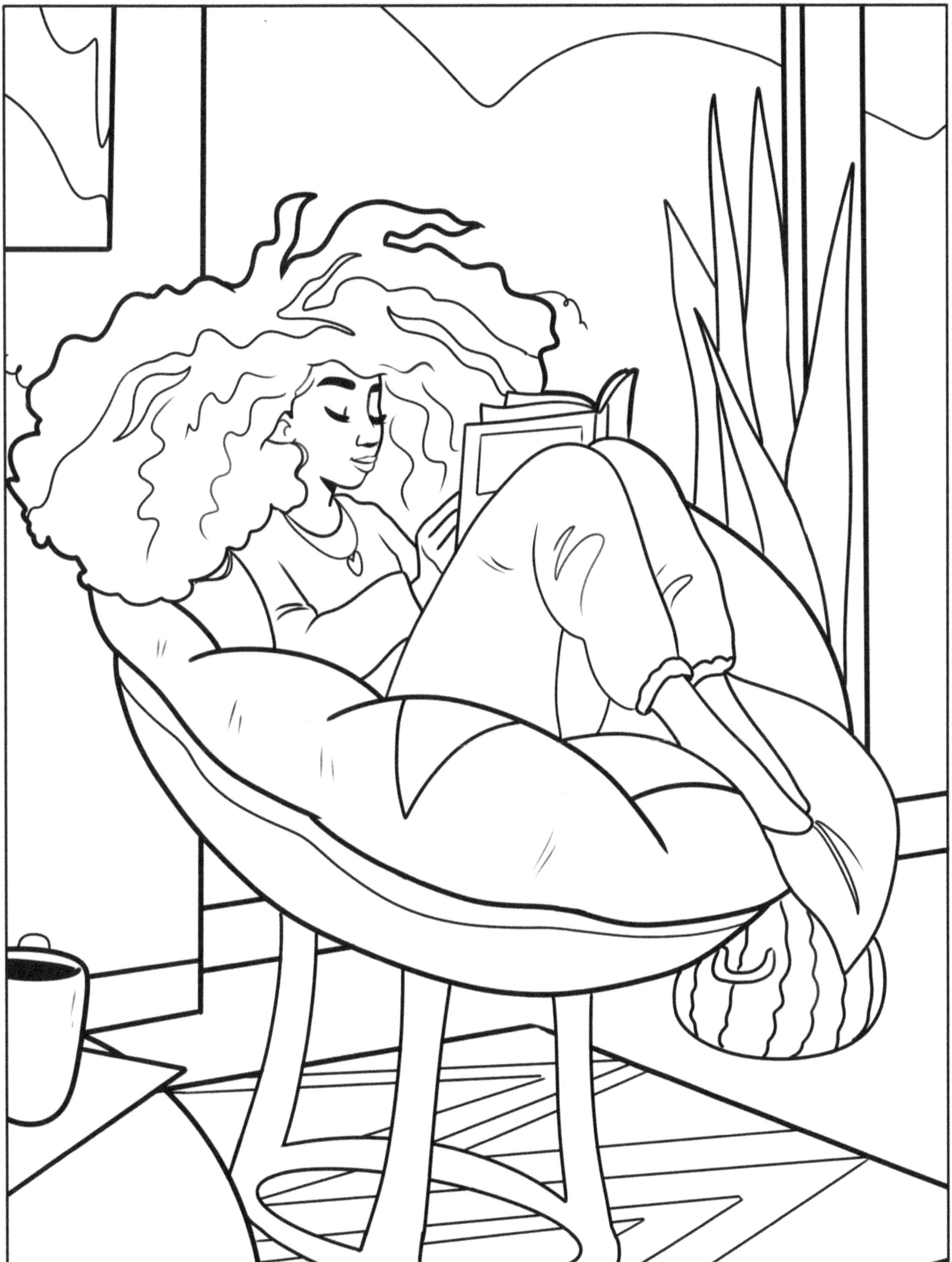

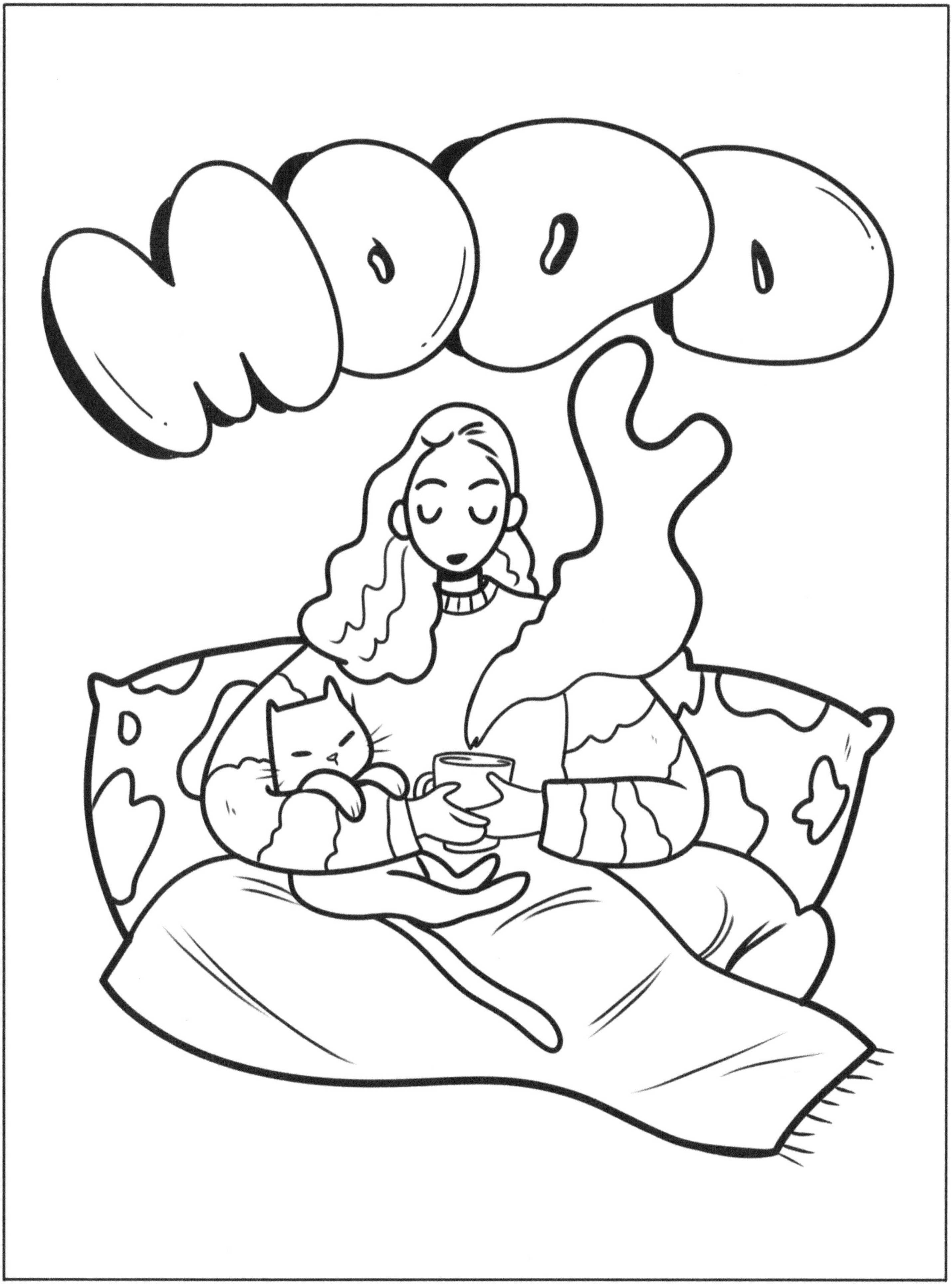
MOOD

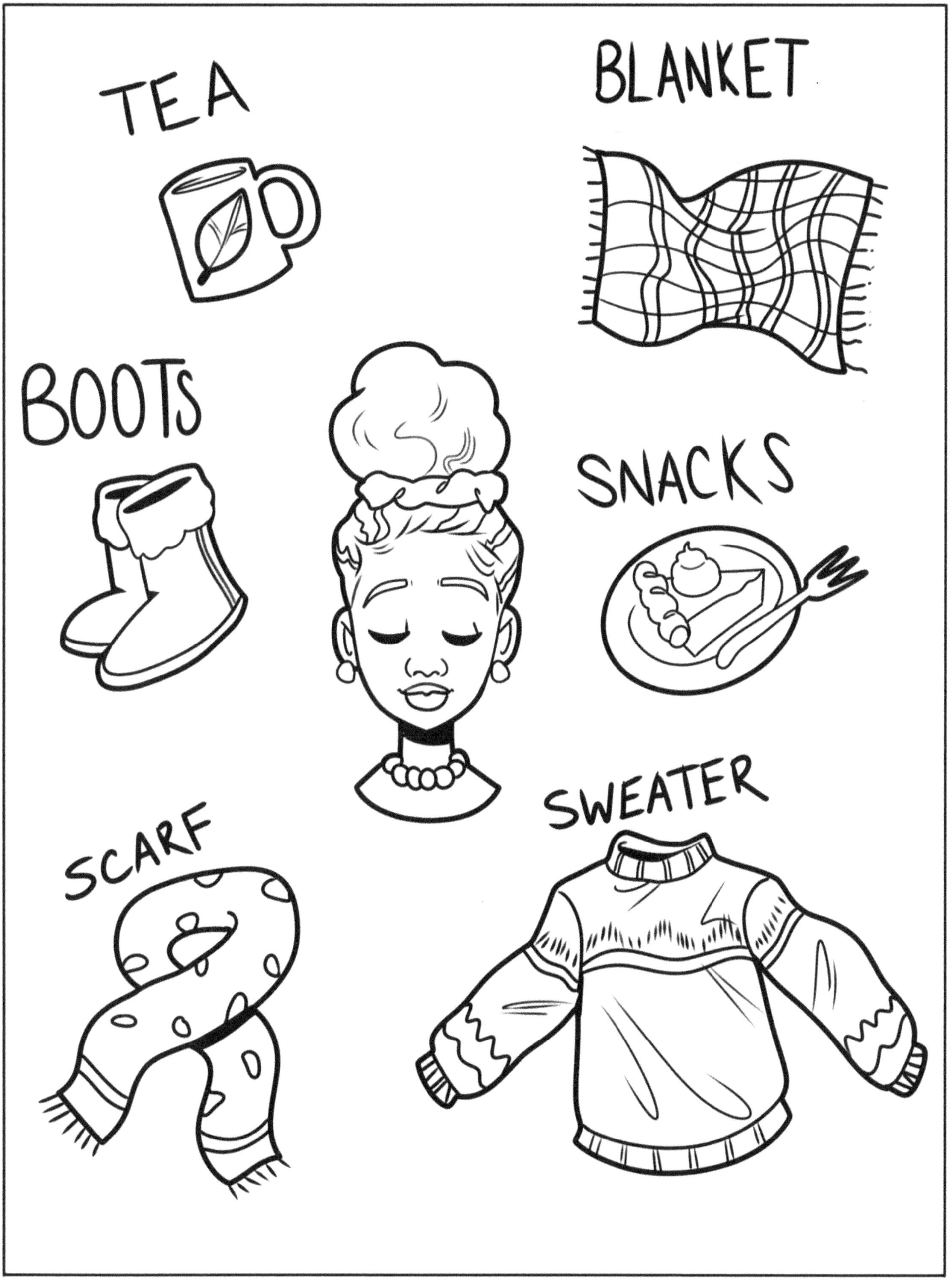
TEA
BLANKET
BOOTS
SNACKS
SWEATER
SCARF

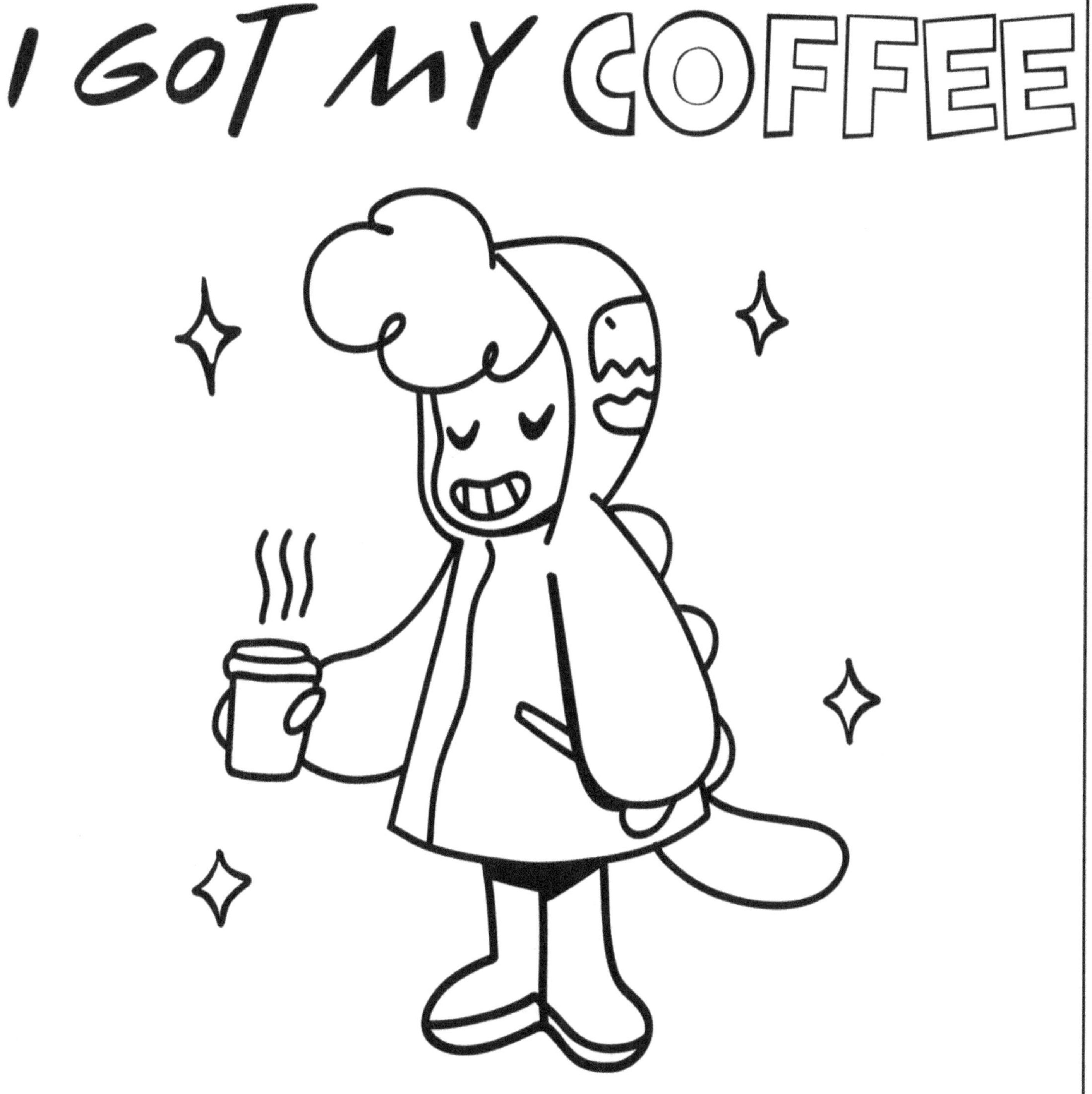
I GOT MY COFFEE

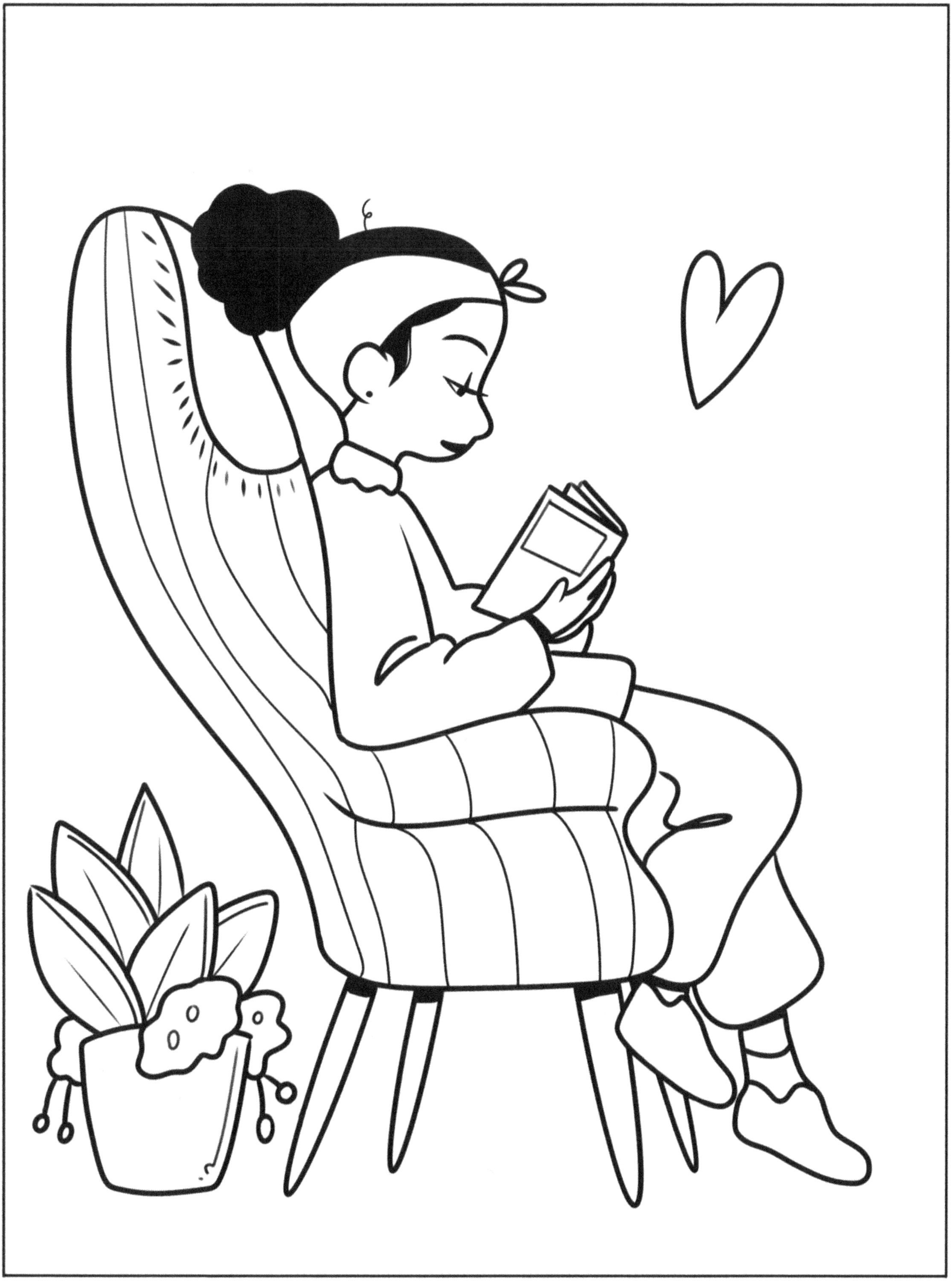

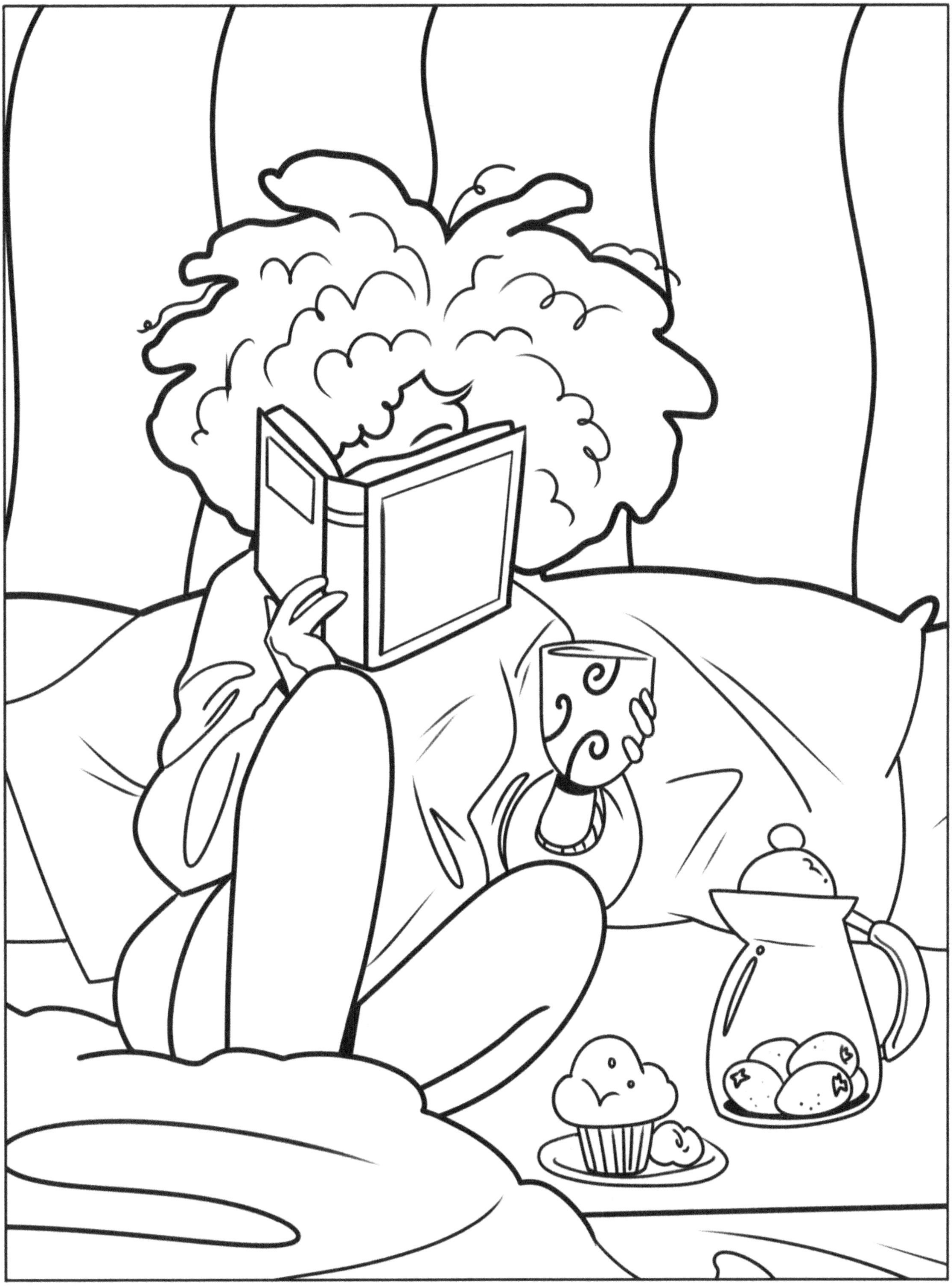

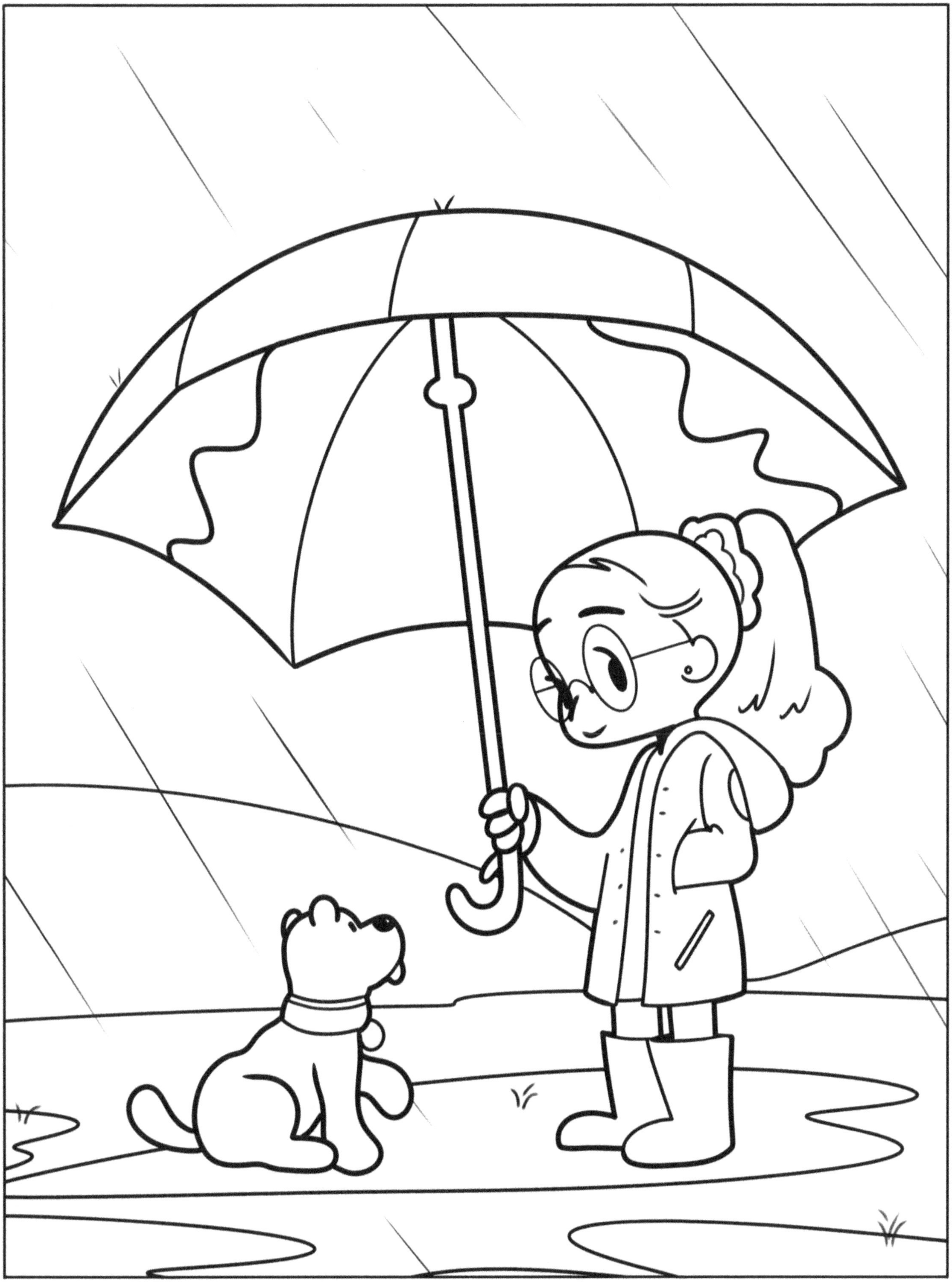

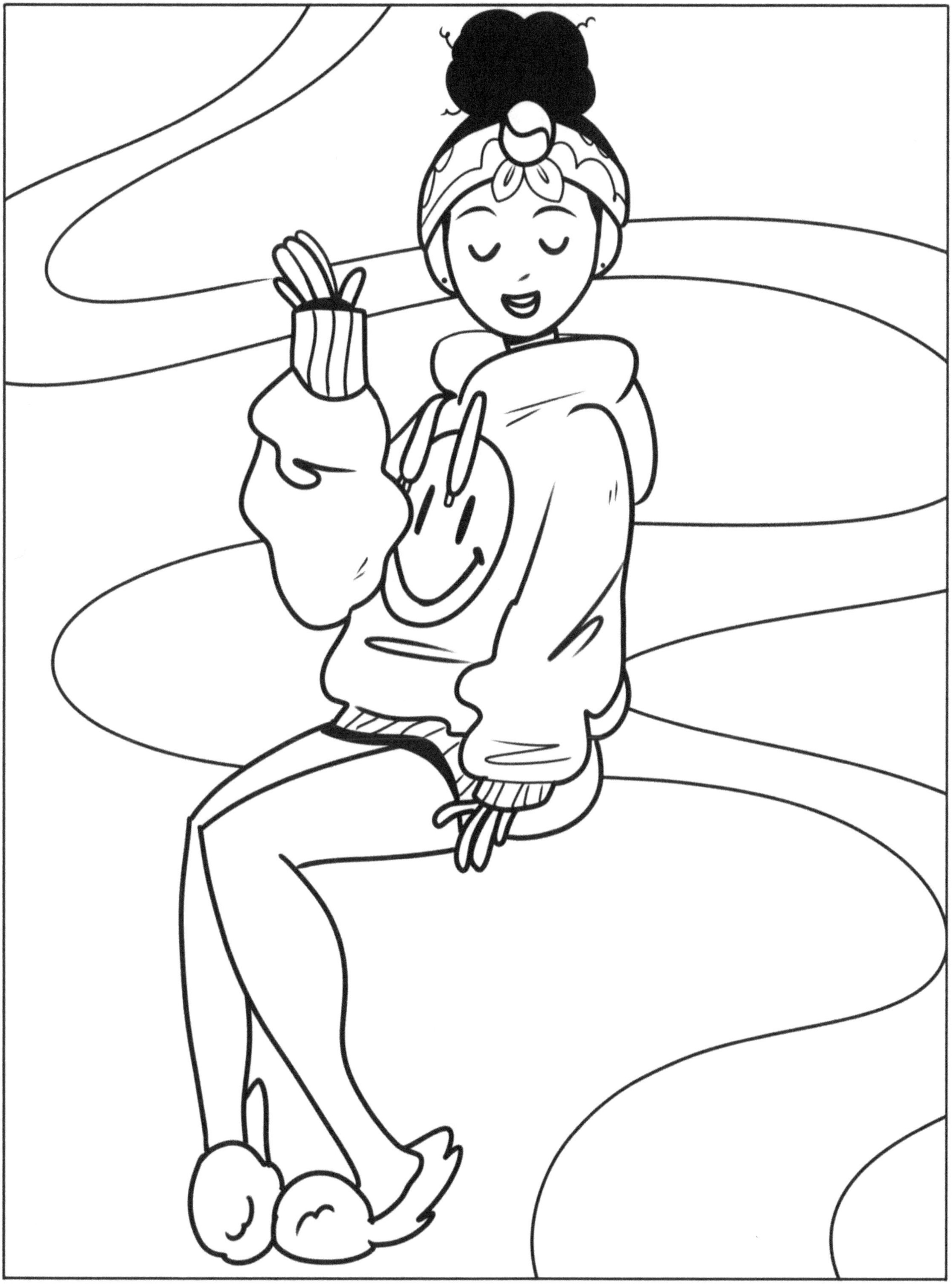

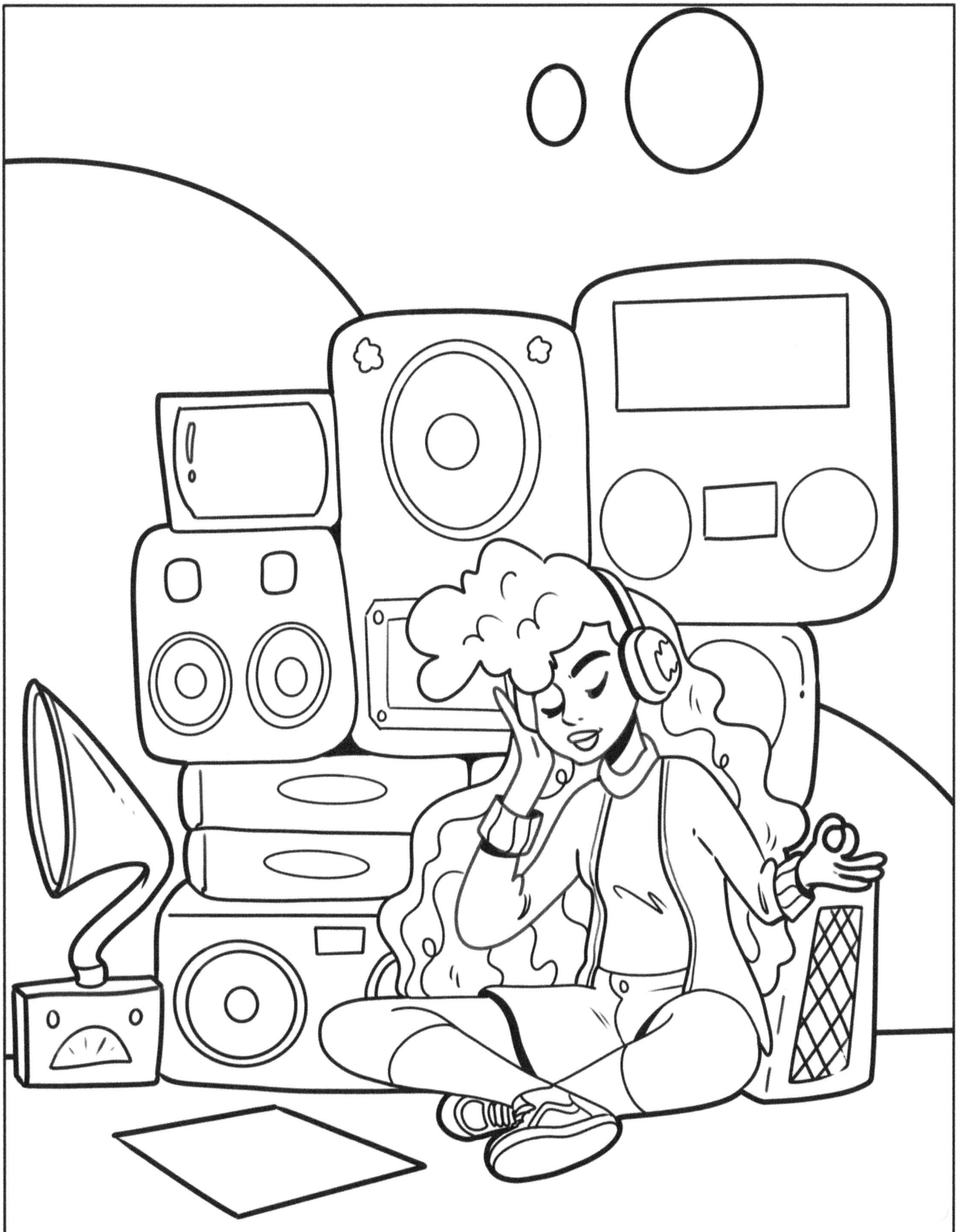

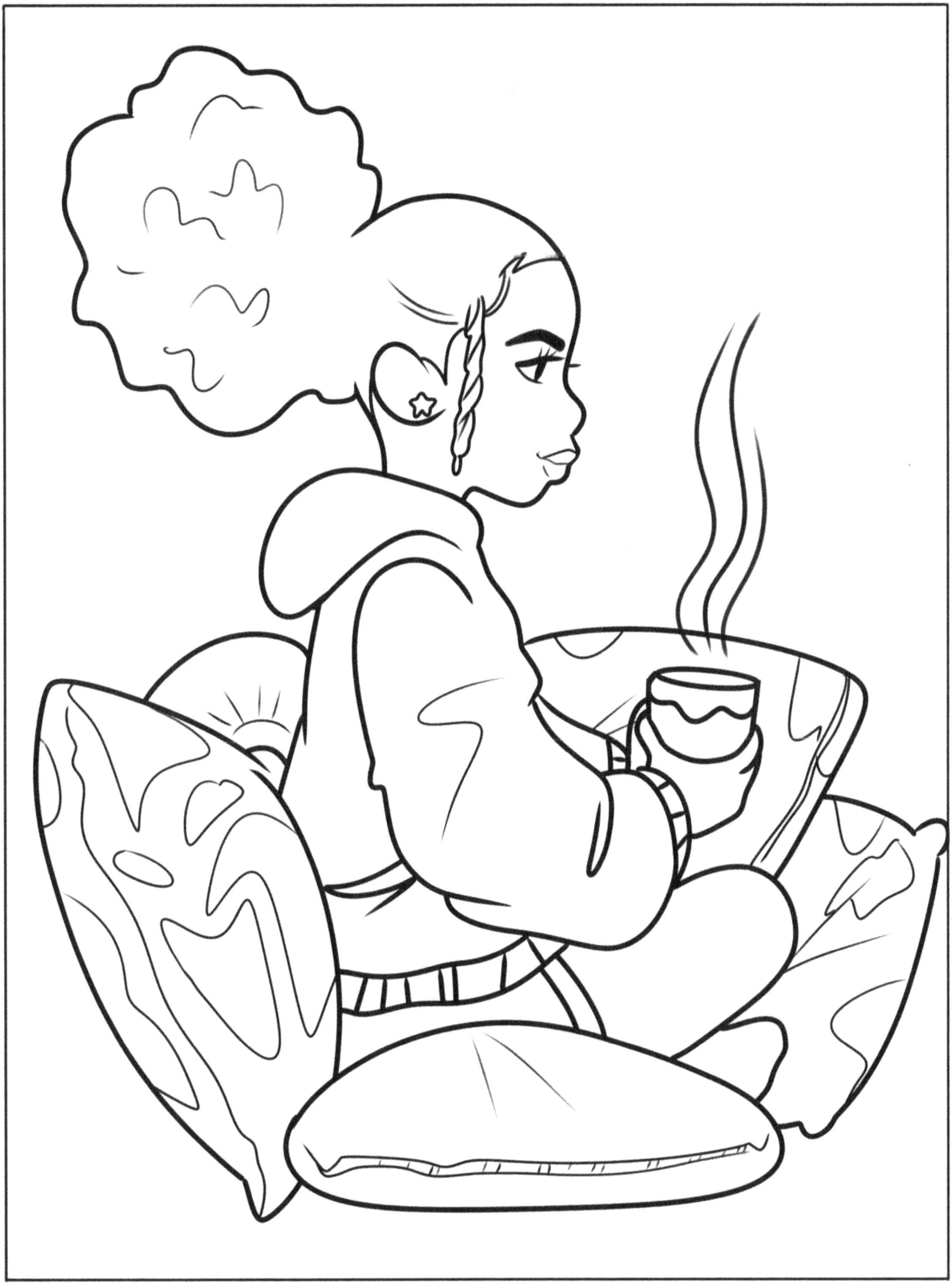

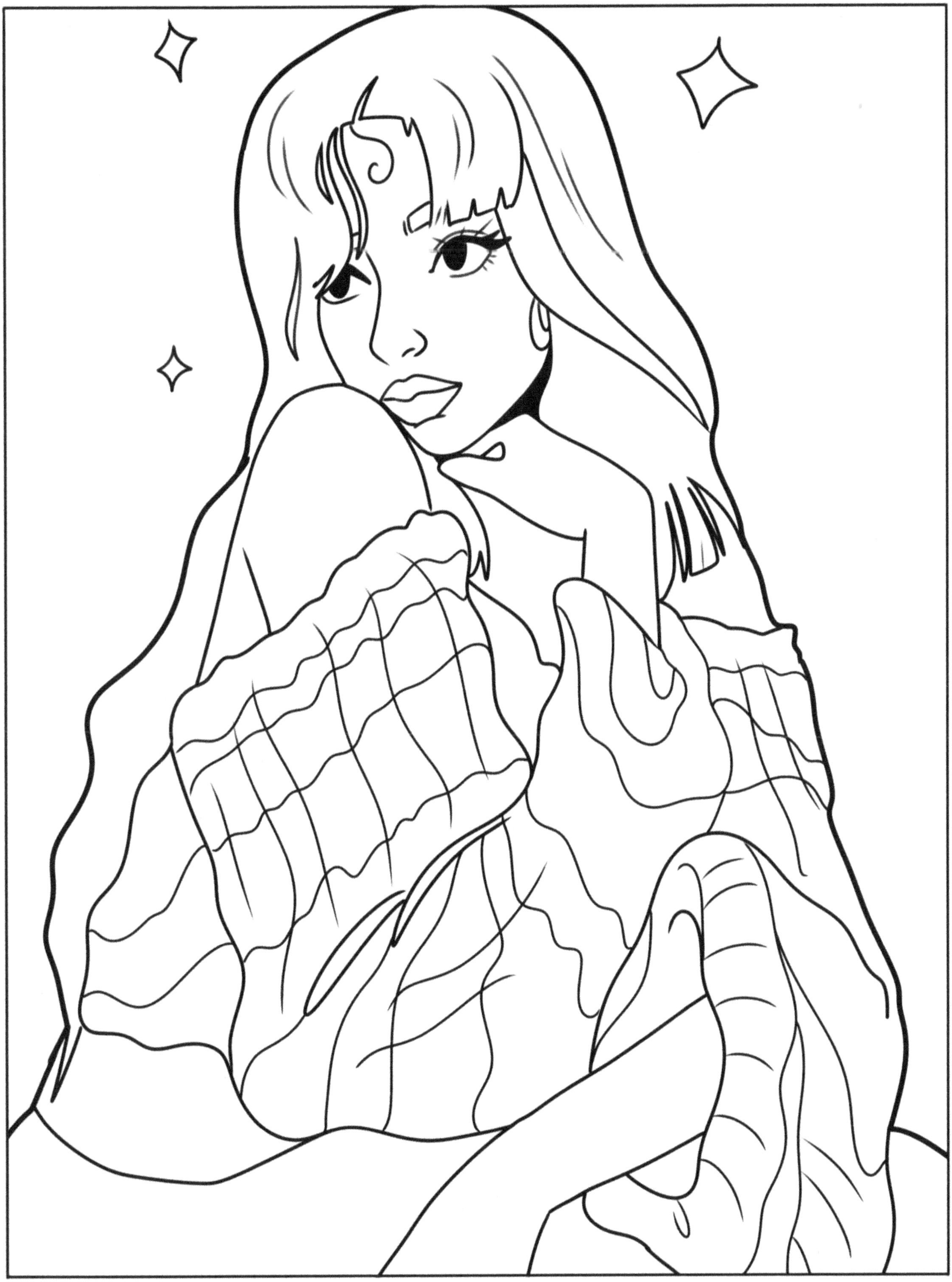

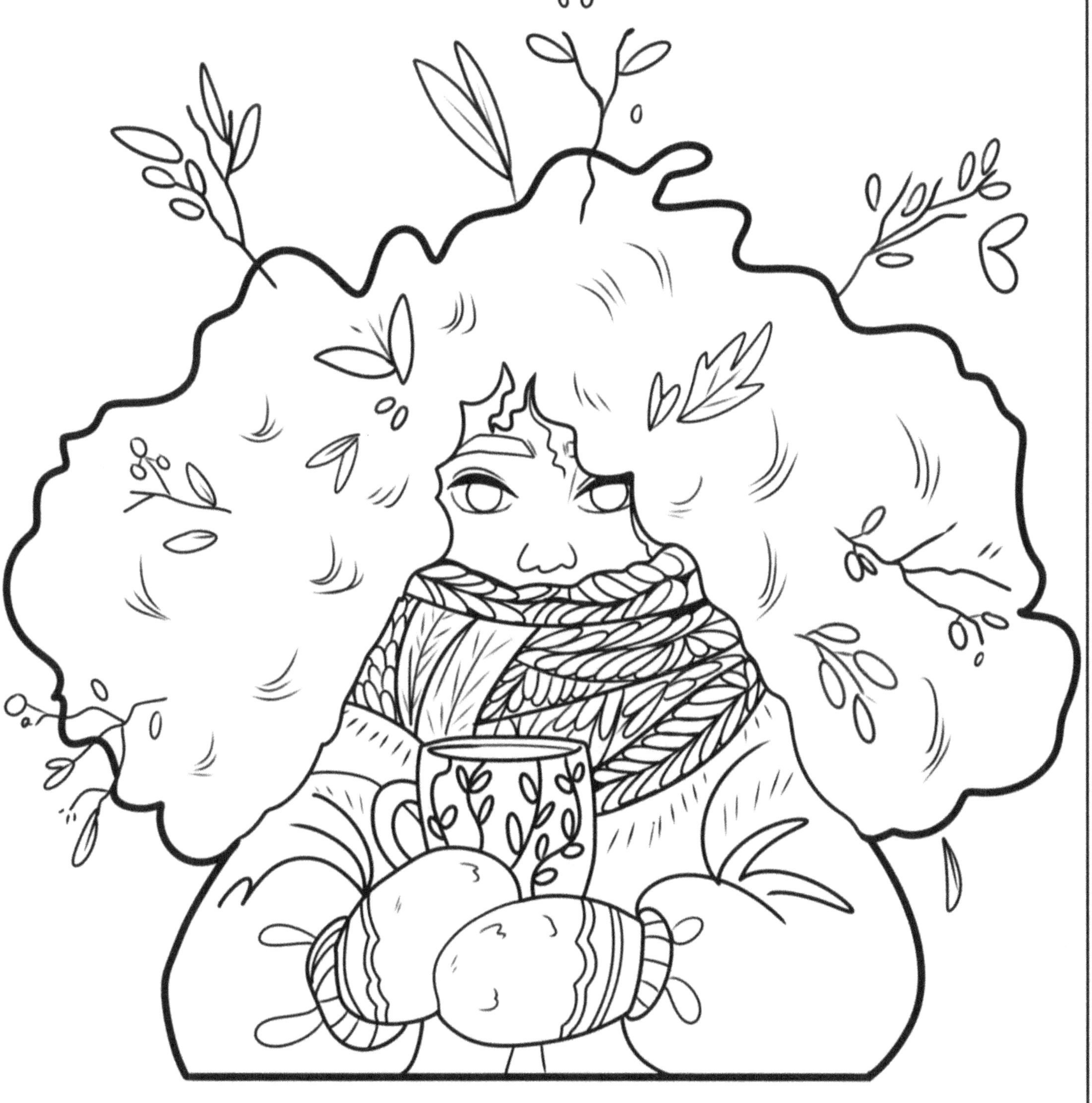

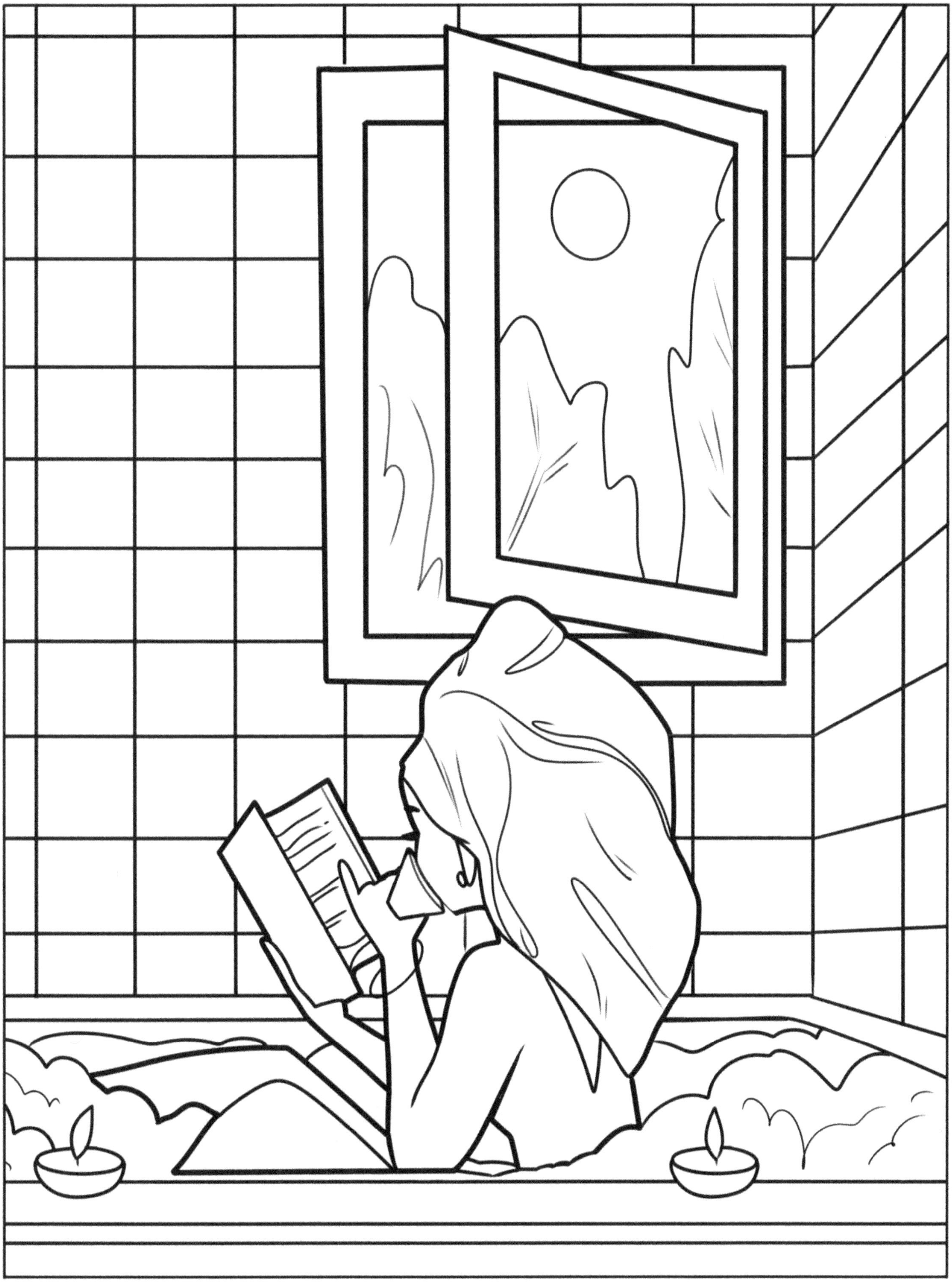

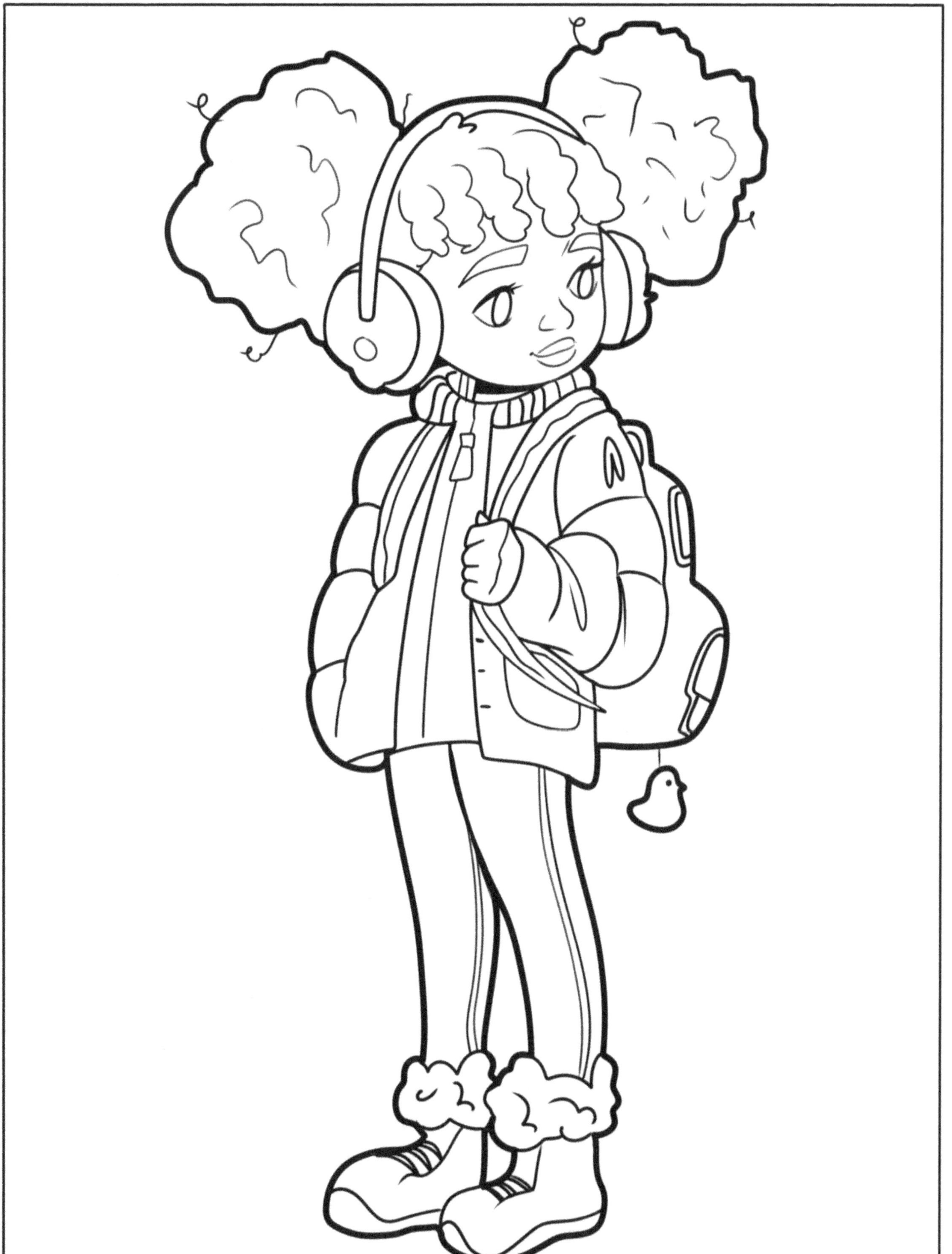

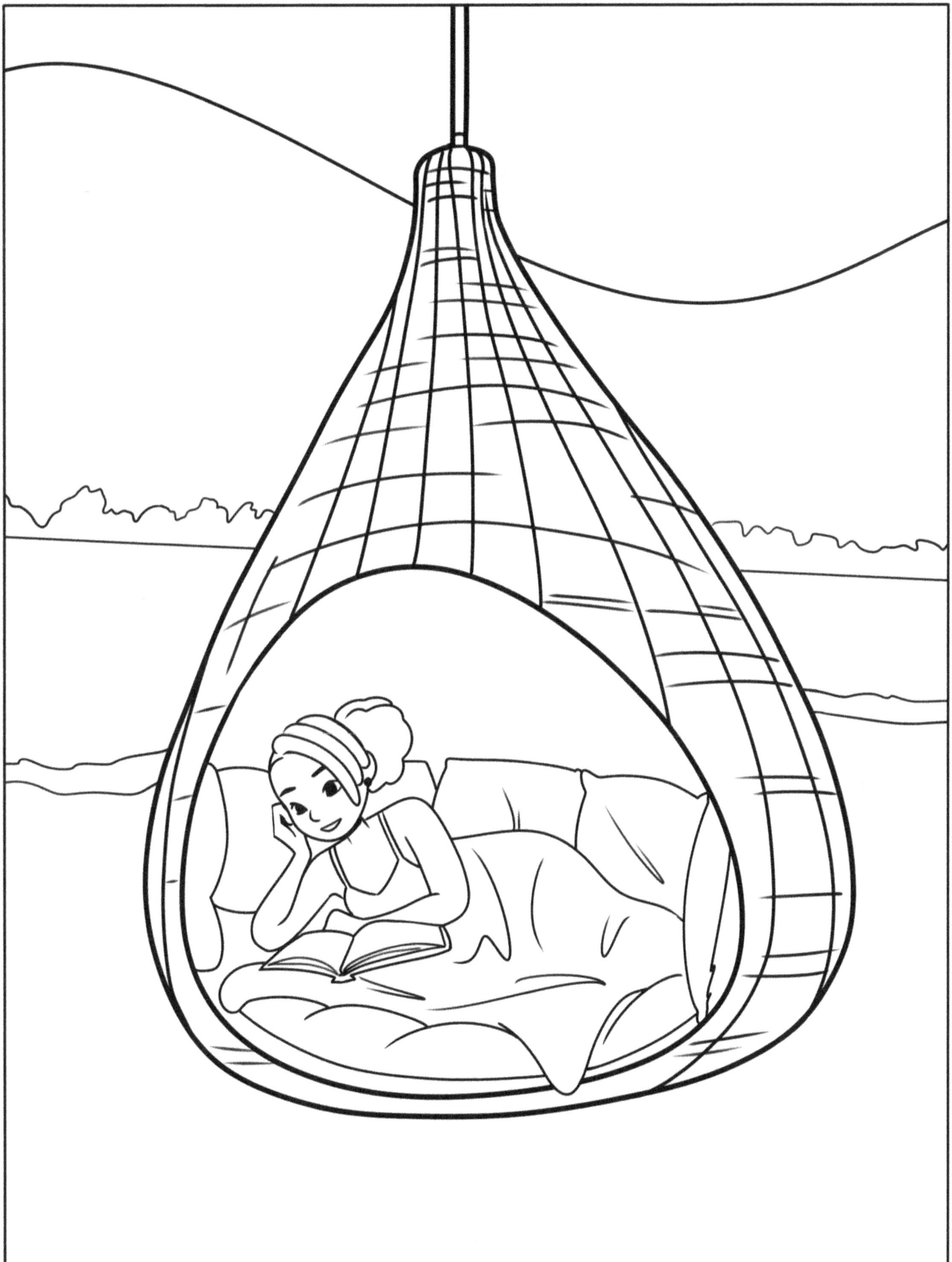

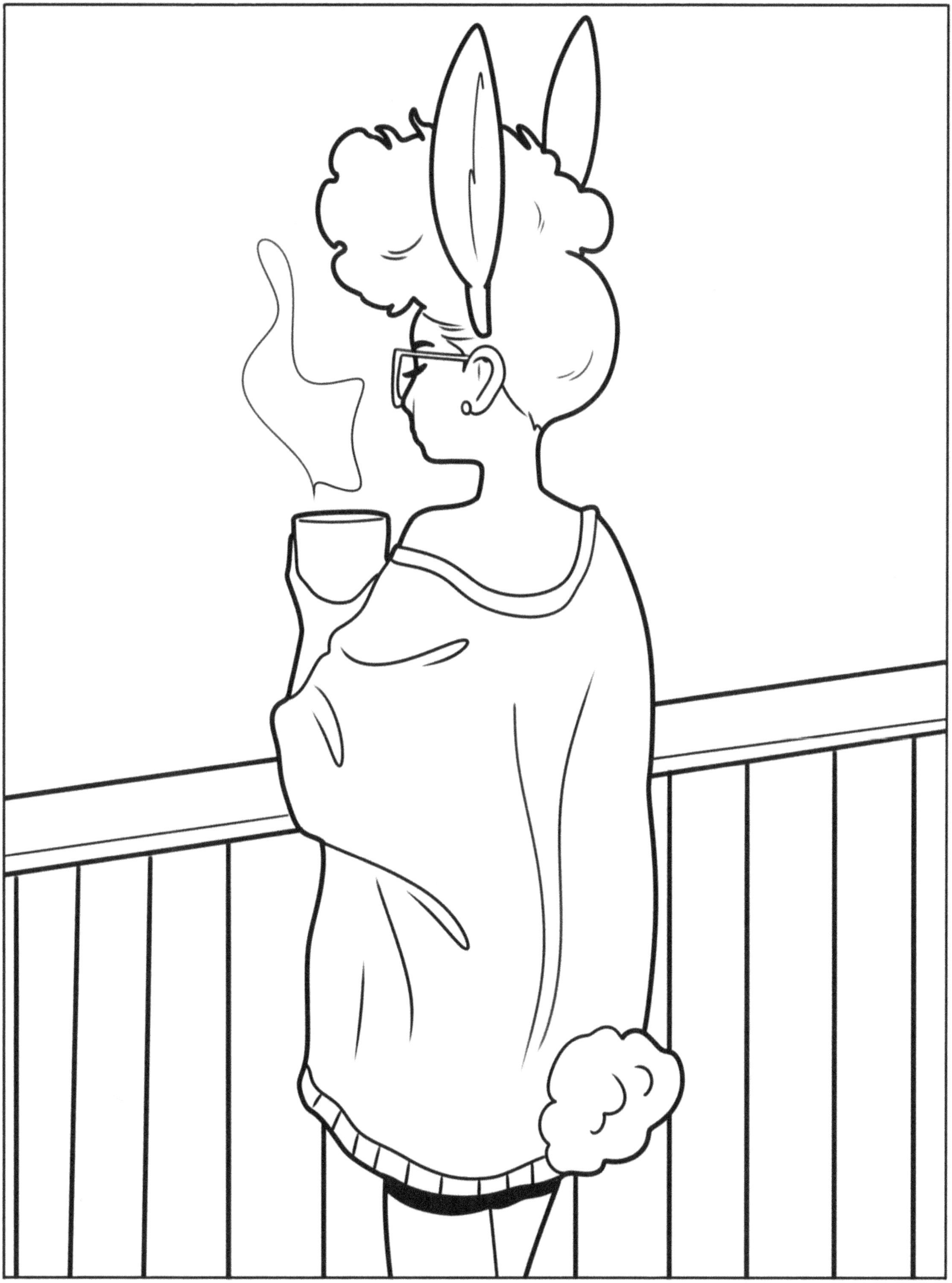

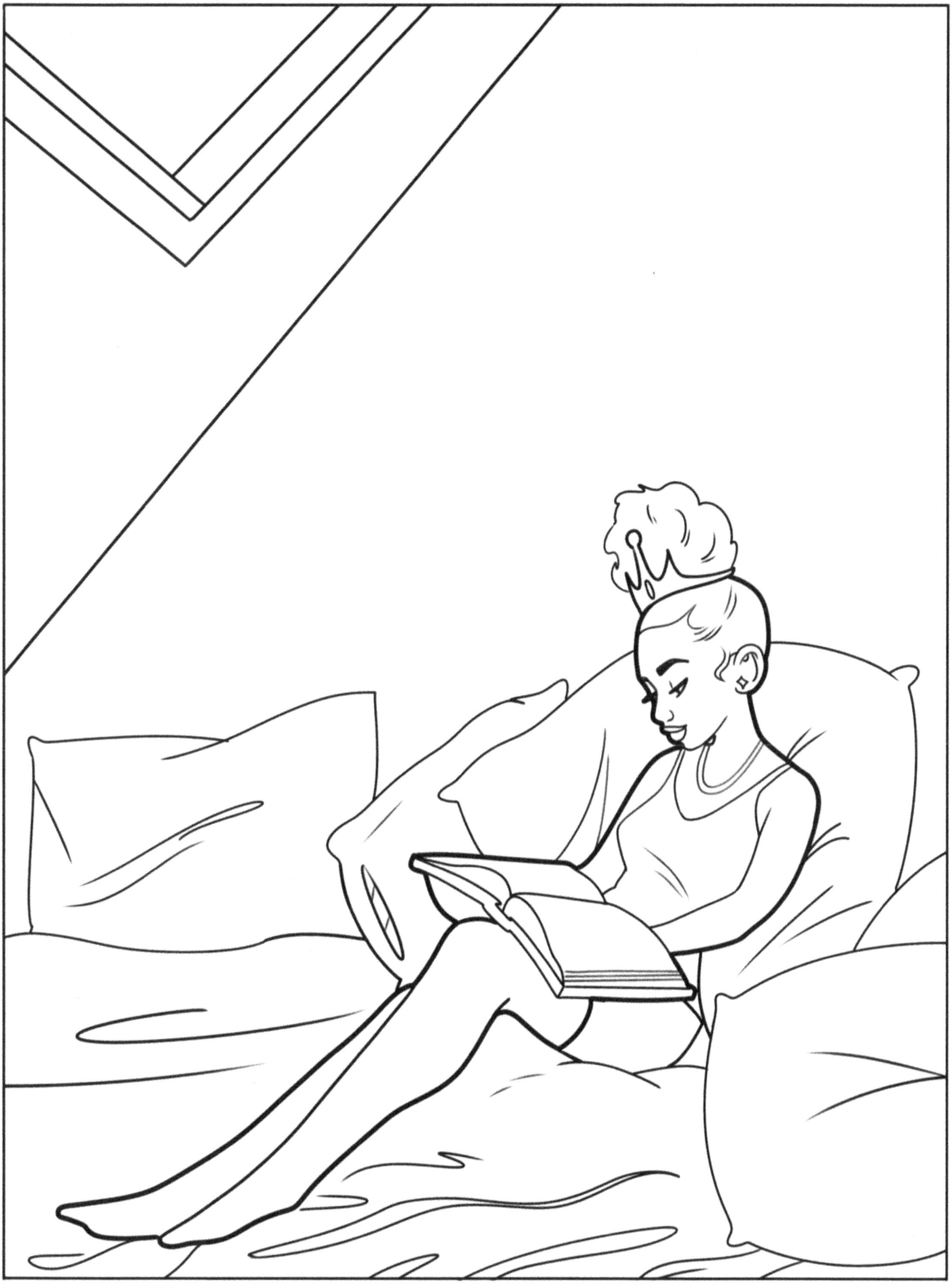

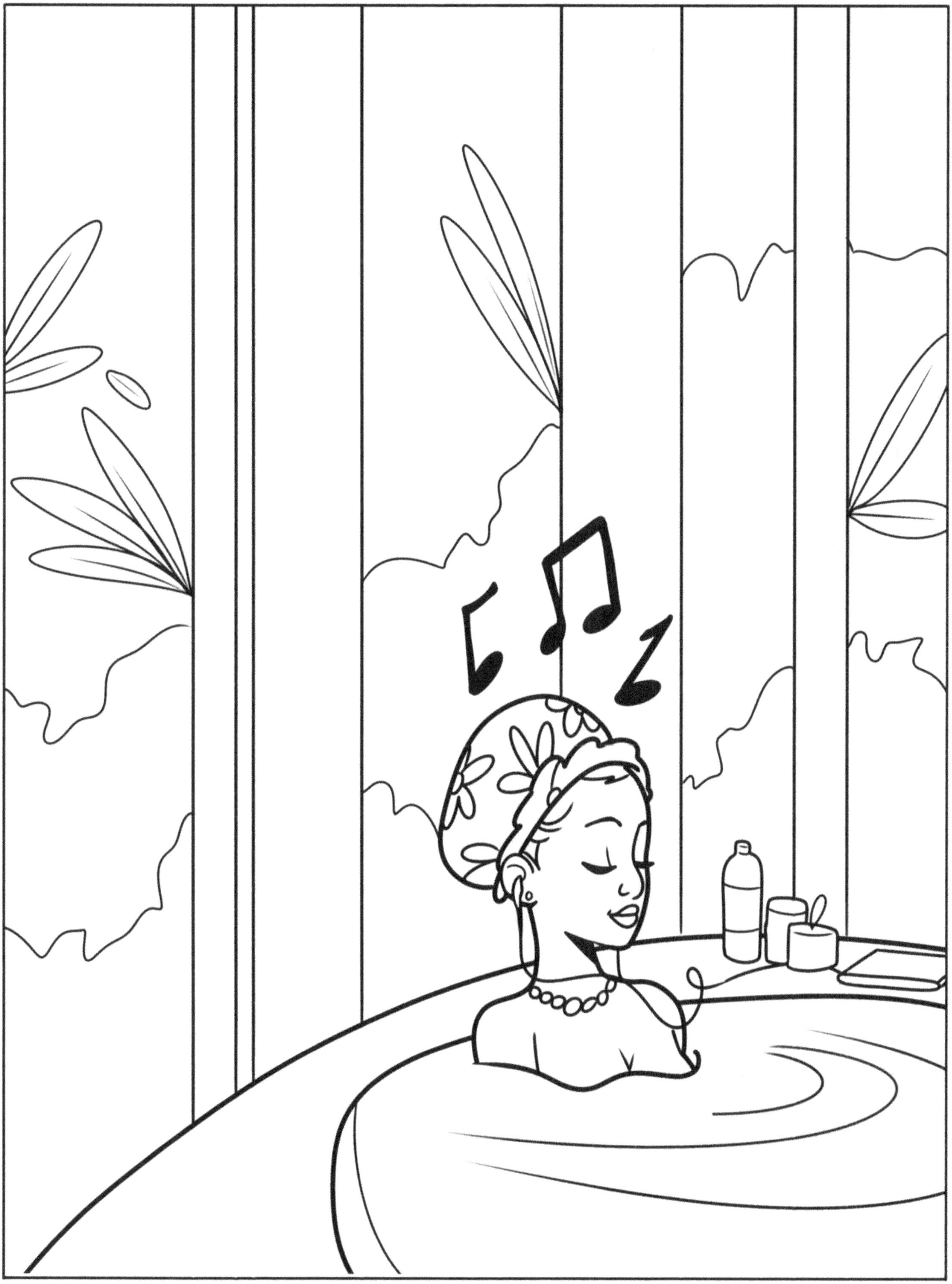

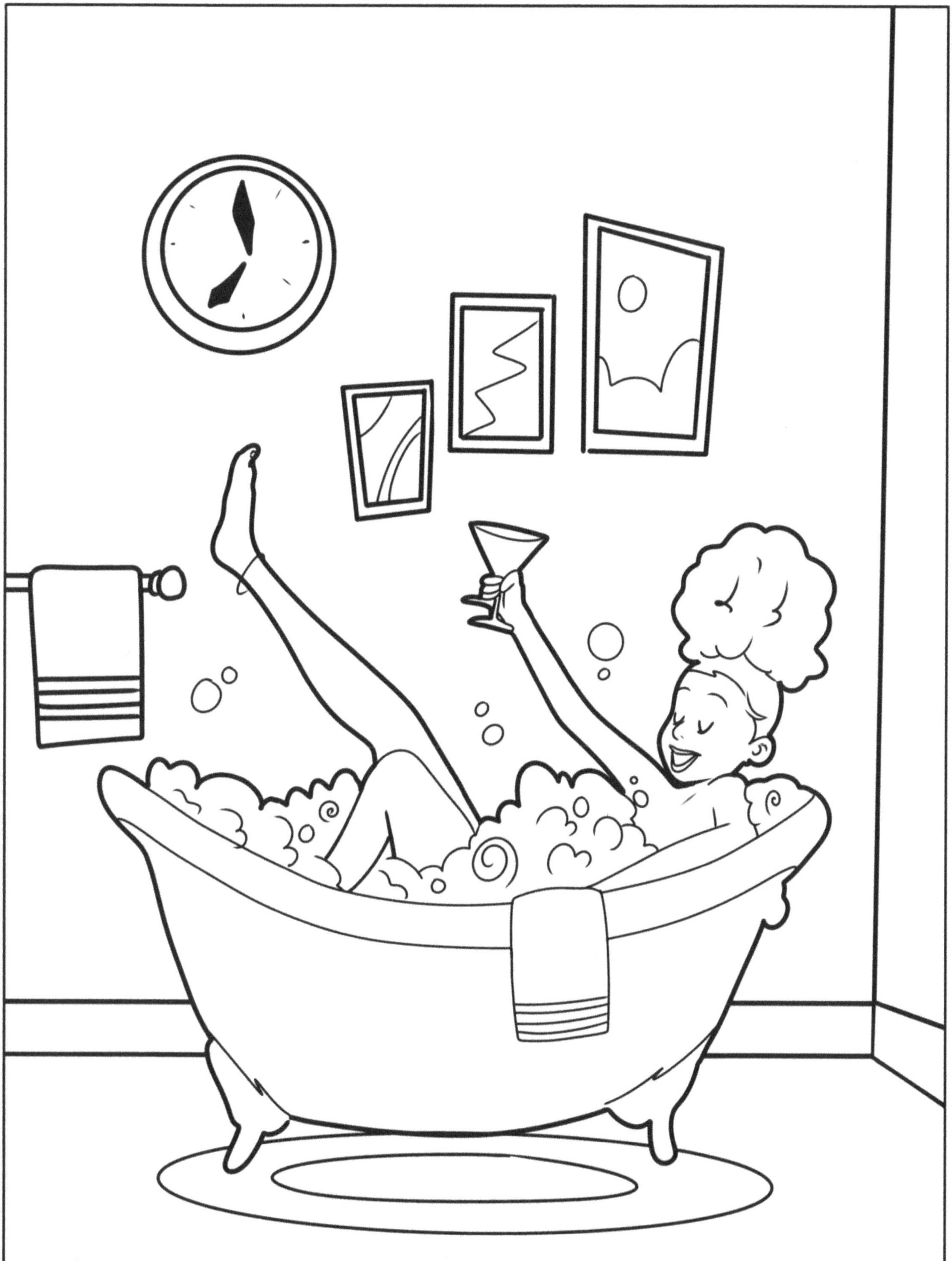

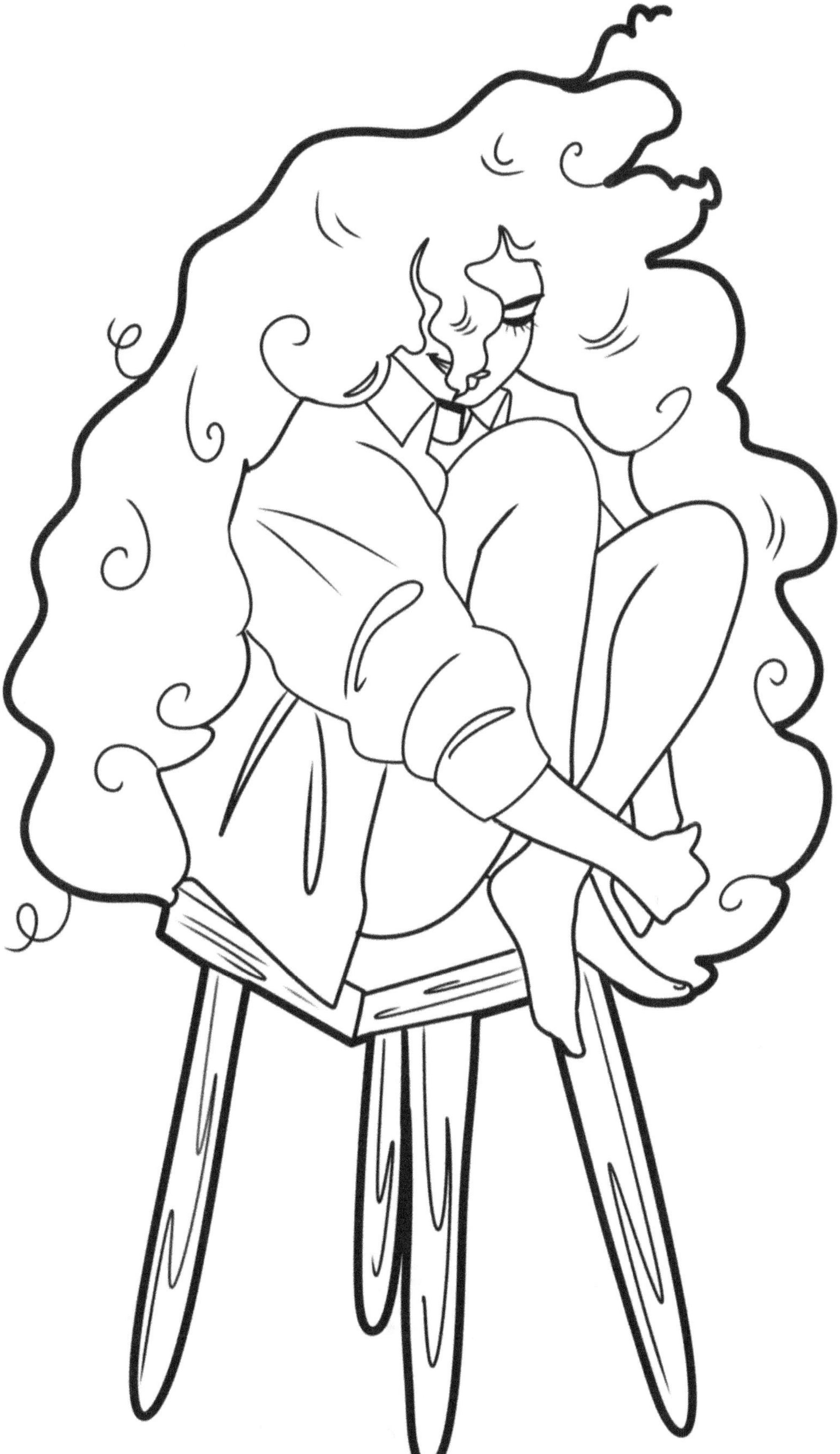

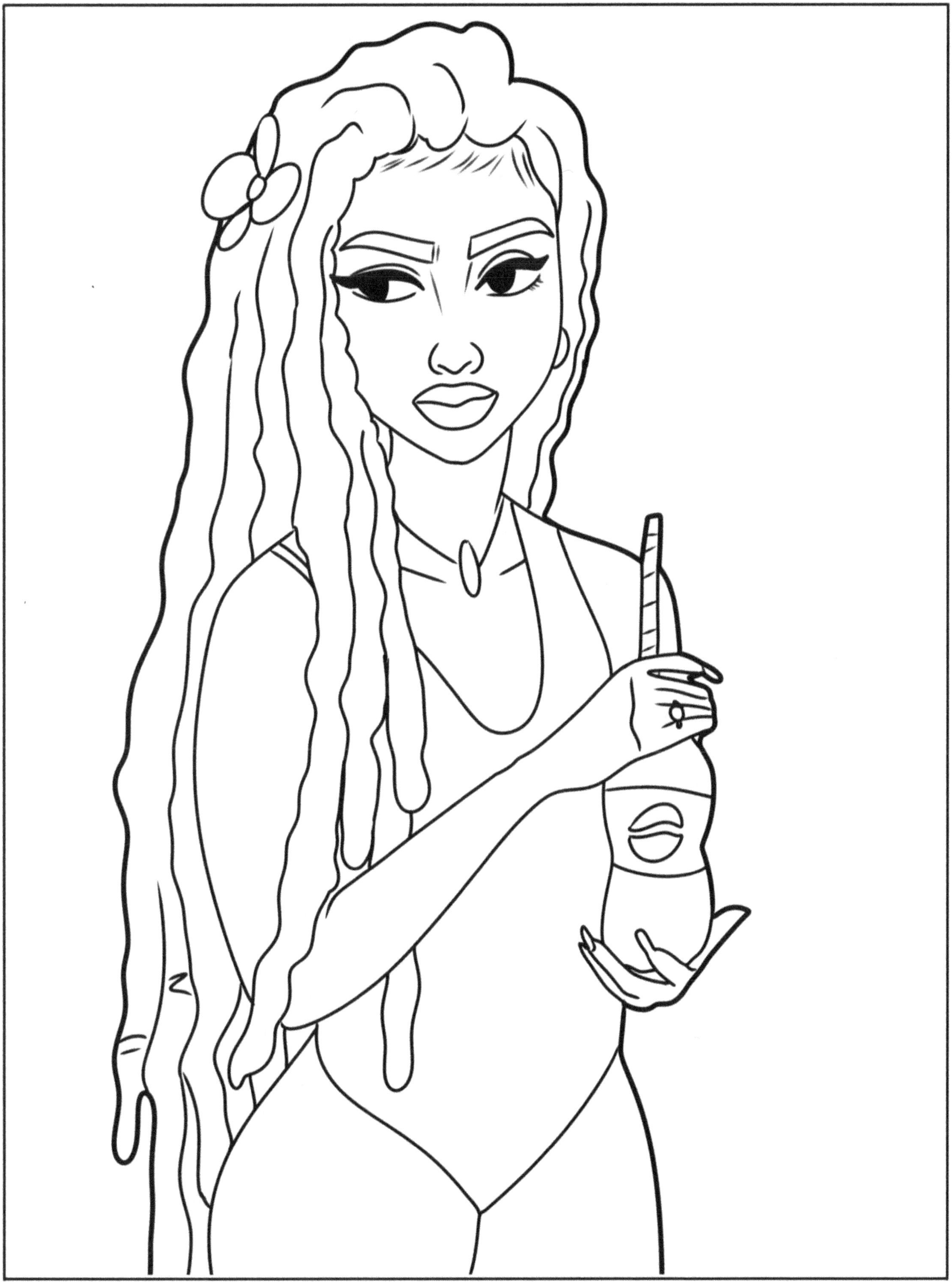

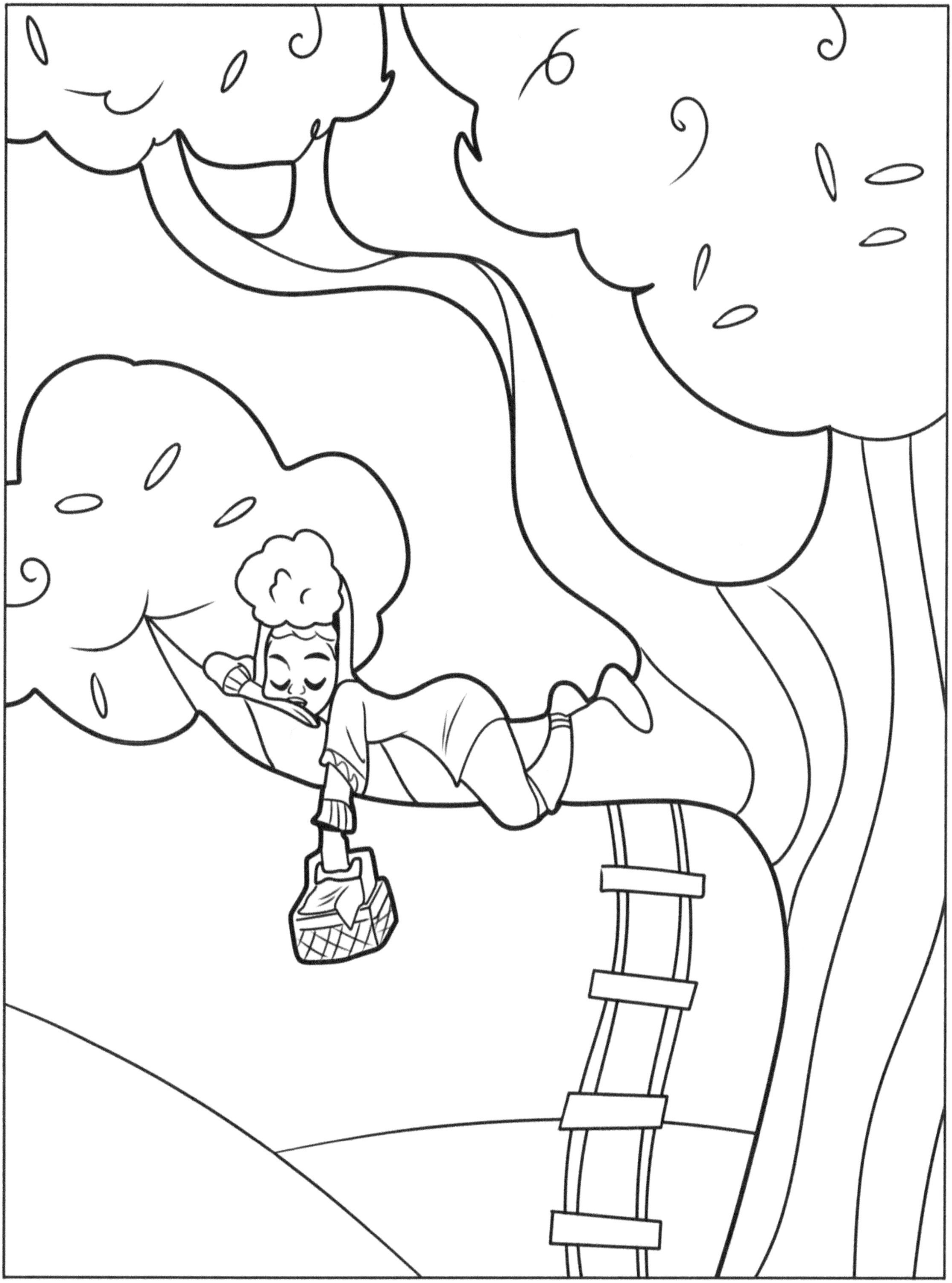

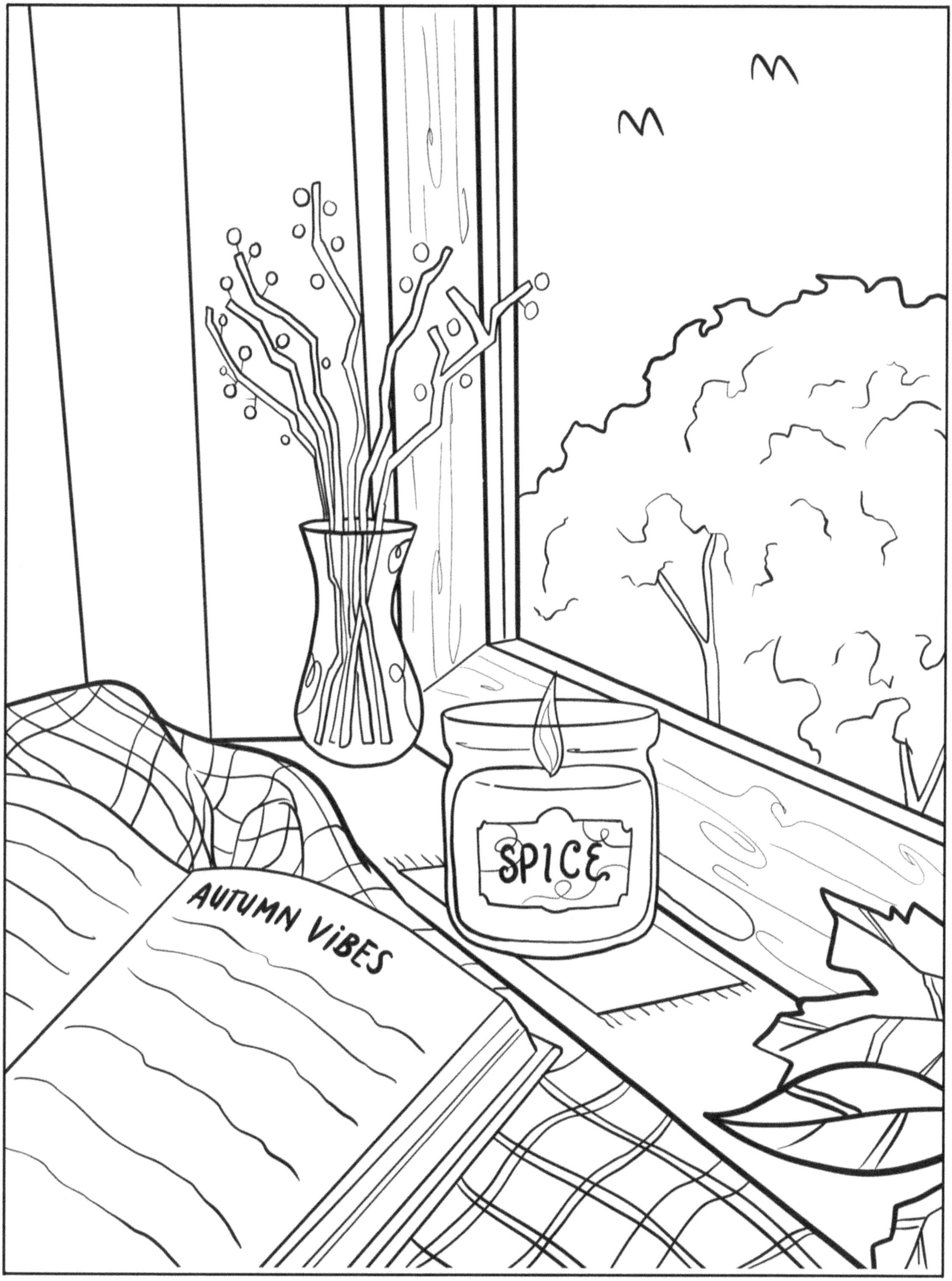
AUTUMN VIBES
SPICE

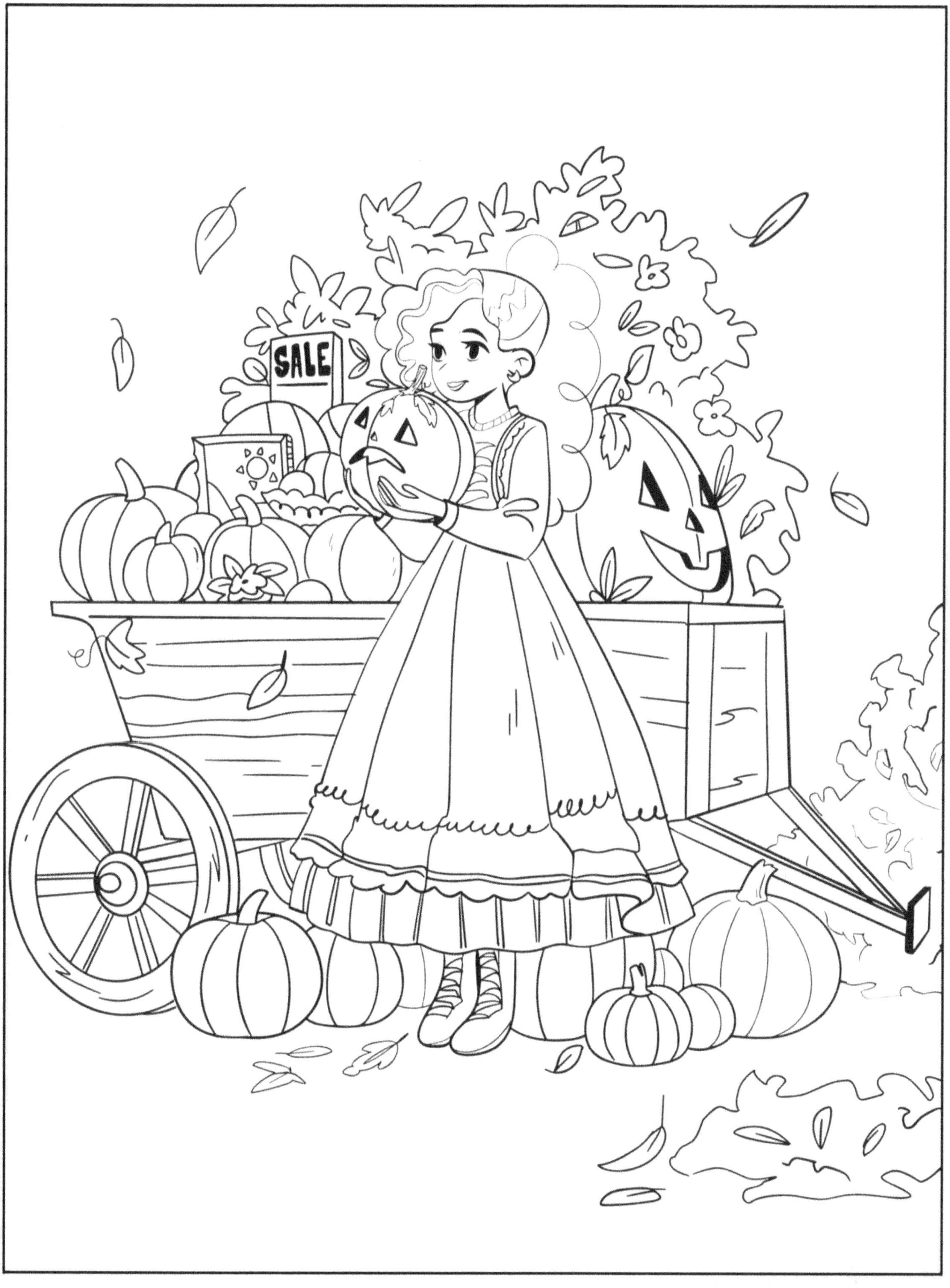
SALE

www.ingramcontent.com/pod-product-compliance
Lightning Source LLC
Chambersburg PA
CBHW080906290526
45795CB00007BA/2430
* 9 7 9 8 8 7 7 0 3 3 6 7 2 *